To my wife, Debbie,
and children, Rachel, Brian, and Daniel,
who have stood with me in
beholding the city.

Contents

CHAPTER 1

Let's Have an Urban Burden!

While ministering in the Flatbush area of Brooklyn, my wife, Debbie, and I lived in an apartment above our flat-roofed, storefront church. It seemed every night a noise came from somewhere to wake us up. Some evenings, the neighbor's barking dog would startle us from our slumber. Other evenings the blaring sounds of rock music from the catering hall on our block shattered our peace. Then there was our next-door neighbor, Max. Max operated an around-the-clock, illegal gambling place. Activities there often disturbed our sleep, and we rang his bell more than once around midnight to ask for a little peace and quiet. One night, Debbie was awakened from sleep by some noise and said, "Matthew, I hear something." Initially I said, "I don't hear anything; go back to sleep." So I did. She continued to hear strange things and got out of bed, thinking to herself, "If it isn't the dog, or the rock music, or Max, it is something else." She again woke me. A little perturbed, I said, "It's just the mice." Sometimes at night they would scurry around and wake us up too. I asked her again to go back to sleep. So I did. Debbie could not rest, however. A third time she woke me up and insisted I look around. I got up and looked out of our bedroom, turned on a hall light, and saw in the middle of our living room floor our television! Instantly I thought, "No mice can move the TV there!" I ran to a hall closet that had a ladder heading straight to the roof. The thief had been going up and down that ladder making the noise Debbie had heard. As I looked up into the closet, I saw only his leg. Then he was gone. We felt violated. Furthermore, the reality hit me that I had been warned three times, but I was slow to believe what was true. I had been robbed, and it would take me some time before I could hear any kind of noise without being struck with fear. Initially, we could not discover anything missing. The police came and checked for fingerprints but we did not think he had taken anything. After the police left, Debbie and I went back to bed, and just as we began to relax after the tension of having a thief in our living room, Debbie said, "The presents!" You see, we had just returned from a trip to the New England states. For the first and last time in our lives we bought some early Christmas presents for our family and had laid them at the foot of the door that the thief had come down. The thief had stolen over $200 worth of gifts. In the morning I walked up the ladder and across the roof and discovered other things the thief had taken. There was actually a trail of small items on the roof and even in the little back yard we had behind our storefront building. As I surveyed the area and picked up some of these items, my heart leaped and my knees began to shake when I saw the cover of an oscillating fan. I realized the danger that God had protected us from as I gazed on that fan cover because the rest of that fan sat upon the dresser in my children's room. Not only had God protected Debbie when she got up to inspect the noise, but the angels of God must have surrounded the two cribs of my small children, Rachel, three years old, and Brian, two years old.

This incident illustrates what is happening in our own nation today. While we sleep in a spiritual slumber, the Devil prowls and destroys our land by devastating our cities. We must wake up! The very thought of urban ministry strikes a negative attitude into the heart of most people. This perspective keeps most Christians from even considering going to a place like New York City or San Francisco or São Paulo. What is your attitude toward the city? What should your outlook be toward the city? Do you have the right urban attitude? The negative urban attitude leads many to not have an urban burden for the great population centers of our world and has led to an alarming lack of urban ministry among Bible-believing Christians.

Humanly speaking, there are many reasons one would want to avoid the city. It is a place of violence, crime, and dirt. Few Christian schools exist there. The city is an expensive place to live. It is too crowded with many people crammed into a small space. The people there are difficult to reach. The city is too big and noisy, too unfriendly and fast-paced, too unstable and transient. There is too much sin in the city. Sinful lifestyles, sinful sights, and sinful sounds plague our cities! Poverty, abuse, loneliness, and hopelessness win the day. Terrorist attacks threaten our security. Why go to a place like that? The city is the Devil's stronghold and a place of great demonic power, but are these reasons to neglect the city and refuse to obey the Great Commission as it relates to the great urban areas of our nation or other nations?

What was Paul's attitude toward the largest city of his day, Rome? Rome was the capital of the fourth world empire. Approximately four million people lived in this cosmopolitan center. On his missionary journeys Paul had seen the tremendous effect of urban ministry in Philippi, Corinth, and Ephesus. Then he said, "I must also see Rome" (Acts 19:21). He was drawn to the hustle and bustle of mighty Rome. It is no coincidence that Paul wrote his masterpiece epistle of Romans to the most influential city in the world. Paul understood that one of the best vehicles for the propagation of the gospel was the city. Since all roads led to Rome, Paul knew that all roads led from Rome and that as the gospel broke into Rome it could also branch out from Rome. He recognized that the city is the ruling head and beating heart of a nation. Paul perceived that since Rome had conquered the world, all the world was in Rome. He had the opportunity to reach the world in one place. If we are going to carry the gospel to our great population centers, we must have the urban attitude Paul had, and not the negative, self-centered, fearful, and often media-created bias that plagues our modern minds. What was Paul's urban attitude?

THANKFULNESS FOR ROME

"To all that be in Rome, beloved of God, called to be saints: Grace to you and peace from God our Father, and the Lord Jesus Christ. First, I thank my God through Jesus Christ for you all, that your faith is spoken of throughout the whole world" (Romans 1:7-8). As Paul considered going to Rome, the first thing he did was to thank God for the Roman believers. His thankfulness did not derive from their "triple A-rated prisons." Neither did his thankfulness stem from his appreciation for the emotional stability of the Roman caesar, for Nero was in power when Paul wrote this letter. Nero would later burn Rome and blame the Christians for his misconduct. Paul's mind was not on the urban negatives, but it was on the people. His heart overflowed with thanks for the people of Rome.

Paul showed his thankful heart for the Roman Christians by *praising* their faith. His urban attitude was one of gratefulness for the saints whose "faith is spoken of throughout the whole world." He could have listed many reasons not to go to Rome, but he focused not upon the negative aspects of the city but upon the people. Likewise, we need to get our minds off the negative features of urban living, and get our hearts on the people!

Read Paul's letters to the churches in the great cities of Philippi, Thessalonica, Corinth, and Ephesus. He experienced traumatic events in each one of those cities, which would have caused the average person never to return to the city; yet he reflected upon his ministry in those cities with joy because he thanked God for the people. While in Philippi, Paul was beaten and thrown into the inner prison of the jail (Acts 16: 19-34). When Paul wrote the church in that city his focus was on the people: "I thank my God upon every remembrance of you" (Philippians 1:3). In Thessalonica, Paul endured a house assault while staying with Jason (Acts 17:1-9). He had to leave the city secretly. When he wrote back to that assembly, he was thankful for the wonderful people with whom he had worked. "We give thanks to God always for you all, making mention of you in our prayers" (I Thessalonians 1:2). Paul feared in Corinth while ministering there. He was threatened and almost beaten before Gallio (Acts 18:1-17), but he maintained an attitude of appreciation for the people of Corinth. "I thank my God always on your behalf, for the grace of God which is given you by Jesus Christ" (I Corinthians 1:4). Paul endured a riot in Ephesus and fought with men who behaved like wild beasts. He wrote back to that church with a thankful heart: "Wherefore I also, after I heard of your faith in the Lord Jesus, and love unto all the saints, cease not to give thanks for you, making mention of you in my prayers" (Ephesians 1:15-16).

If we focused upon the people, perhaps more of us would desire to go to a modern-day Rome. The people of Rome had a mighty faith! As I ponder a place such as New York City, I must not focus on the negative facets of city life. My focus is on the eight million people who need the Lord Jesus Christ. Multitudes from every corner of the earth live in New York City—people who love the Lord, people with great faith, people who live for Christ in spite of incredible trials and pain.

Paul also demonstrated his thankfulness for the Roman saints by *praying* for them. "For God is my witness, whom I serve with my spirit in the gospel of his Son, that without ceasing I make mention of you always in my prayers" (Romans 1:9). Paul prayed unceasingly for the believers at Rome. No wonder he ended up going! Do you pray for our nation's cities? Do you pray for the great cities of our world? We should be praying that God would bring a revival to our cities. A revival in a major city would shake any nation. Will you pray for God to send laborers into our cities? Will you pray for God to give you a willing heart to minister in our cities?

HOMESICKNESS FOR ROME

Paul had a spirit of longing to be in Rome. "For I long to see you" (Romans 1:11*a*). Literally, Paul was homesick for the city that ruled the world! Most people can relate to being homesick. It is that feeling of emptiness and loneliness in being away from those you love. This same Greek word is used to describe Paul's longing for heaven (II Corinthians 5:2), and Peter used it to describe his longing for God's Word (I Peter 2:2). Paul had this feeling of homesickness for the capital of the world in order to spread the gospel. I can understand being homesick for heaven or for home, but have you ever been homesick for a huge city? Paul had been to Ephesus, to Corinth, to Philippi, to Thessalonica, and to Athens. His burden for the city had grown as he saw the multitudes of people without the Savior. Paul was now homesick for a place he had never been. He was a metropolitan missionary with an urban burden. I like to call him an urban jungle rat. He felt a great urge to invade Rome with the same message he had carried elsewhere. Oh, may God give us this attitude.

Paul's spirit was burdened for the believers in Rome. He wanted to be in their midst. "That I may come unto you with joy by the will of God, and may with you be refreshed" (Romans 15:32). Paul could never have imagined what he would endure in traveling to Rome. God allowed him to make it there, shackled in chains, soggy from shipwreck, scared by a snakebite, but alive and "strong in the Lord, and in the power of his might." Paul arrived in Rome ready to spread the gospel even though he was a prisoner.

Why was Paul homesick for the believers in Rome? Did he long to see all the famous sights of this wealthy city? No, Paul had a desire to *render a gift.* "For I long to see you, that I may impart unto you some spiritual gift, to the end ye may be established" (Romans 1:11). Paul longed to minister to the Roman Christians with the spiritual gifts God had given him. Paul desired to preach and teach in the power of God's Spirit in order to edify and establish them in the faith and encourage them to use their spiritual gifts for God's glory. He was homesick to see them rooted in love and built up in the faith.

A key principle in being used in ministry is to be yourself. Paul knew his effectiveness was greatest when he served God and others with the gifts he had been given. Believers in our cities are in desperate need of instruction in the faith. Cities are areas of amazing religious confusion, moral perversion, and spiritual emptiness. Many in our cities are unstable. They need to be established by Spirit-filled men and women willing to go and serve in the areas in which they are gifted. Even though the Roman believers had great faith, they still were not fully established in their faith. For this reason, Paul longed to see them.

Paul also longed for Rome because he knew he would *receive a blessing.* "That is, that I may be comforted together with you by the mutual faith both of you and me" (Romans 1:12). Paul wanted to go to Rome because he knew the believers would encourage him. When we go to minister the gospel, we are always the one most blessed. Many people think something bad will happen if they venture to a big city, but I tell you, there is a blessing in ministering to souls who need the Lord.

We met Dorothy and her family through door-to-door visitation. She came to New York from Jamaica, West Indies. She was so blessed by coming to our church that she began cooking for us every Sunday. She would give us oxtail, escovitch fish, stewed chicken, macaroni and cheese, all Jamaican style. One of my favorite things about New York City is all the ethnic food, and Dorothy could cook with the best! Often when our refrigerator was empty, the phone would ring and she would be on the line telling us to come pick up some food that would last for a least two days. What a joy in ministering to people who love the Lord!

Paul also believed that in Rome he would *reap a harvest.* "Now I would not have you ignorant, brethren, that oftentimes I purposed to come unto you, (but was let hitherto,) that I might have some fruit among you also, even as among other Gentiles" (Romans 1:13). Paul knew that souls in Rome would be saved. He might have to go out on a limb, but that is where the fruit is the most ripe! He knew the God of the gospel was great, and there was fruit to be plucked! There is fruit to be picked in cities like New York, São Paulo, Chicago, or Lagos, but we must go. There will be no harvest if no one goes.

Francisco walked into our church service one morning with a black eye and a fresh scar across his forehead. At the end of the service I asked if he knew the Lord Jesus Christ as his Savior. His face lit up and he responded, "Yes." The Lord had saved him just five days previous to his visit to our church. I then asked his wife, Patricia, if she knew she was a child of God. "No," she replied. I had one of the ladies in our church lead Patricia to faith in Jesus, and I discipled them. I discovered that Francisco had been hanging out in drug areas getting high and neglecting his wife and small child. One of those nights he was mugged, cut up, and almost killed. The Lord had his attention, and he was saved soon after that. In his search for a church they came to Parkway Baptist Church in Rosedale, Queens. Yes, there is fruit in urban ministry!

INDEBTEDNESS FOR ROME

"I am a debtor both to the Greeks, and to the Barbarians; both to the wise, and to the unwise" (Romans 1:14). Every Christian ought to have a sense of obligation to give the gospel to every man. These inspired words of Paul also say something significant about our attitude toward the capital cities of nations, the population centers of our world. Paul knew the whole world was represented in Rome: Jews, Greeks, and Barbarians. This represents all men. Do you have a burden for the multitudes of Jewish people in the great cities of our world? Do you have a burden for people who are different in culture from you? The city is the meeting of the nations. We have an occasion in the city to reach the world in one place! Not only were all nations of men represented, but all classes of men were represented. There were wise and unwise, educated and uneducated. Paul believed he could reach and have fruit among all cultures, all classes, and all colors of men. We must have a heart to go into all the world and preach the gospel to every creature.

READINESS FOR ROME

"So, as much as in me is, I am ready to preach the gospel to you that are at Rome also" (Romans 1:15). The root word for "ready" *(thumos)* is literally a boiling heat, or passion. The primary root is "to sacrifice." Paul was burning with eagerness to preach the gospel in Rome and to announce the good news in the capital city of his world. He had a passion and heart to sacrifice for the city. Rome was a city full of fish, and Paul was a fisher of men. He was excited; he had a ready spirit. Paul was ready for Rome! Are you ready to do such a thing? Are you ready to be a living sacrifice in a great city of your world? It is exciting and joyous to preach in the city. Is there a passion in your heart for the city; is there a flaming zeal to preach the gospel? Are you boiling to be a witness for Christ? We need to have the kind of eagerness and desire that Paul had. Paul possessed a passionate attitude that overcame all cultural differences and overleaped all racial barriers.

The New York Fire Department demonstrated heroic readiness on September 11, 2001. While thousands ran from the smoking Twin Towers, firefighters from all over the city ran to the fire. They successfully evacuated twenty-five thousand people from the Towers in an hour of time. It was the greatest evacuation effort in the history of New York City. A powerful photograph of firefighters from the Brooklyn Heights Ladder Company 118 that summarized their passion to save lives appeared on the front of the *New York Daily News* on October 5. This sobering picture was taken high atop the *Watchtower* headquarters looking down upon the famed Brooklyn

Bridge. The only vehicle on the bridge was Ladder Company 118 racing into Manhattan. Behind the Brooklyn Bridge the fire in the doomed Twin Towers raged out of control. A firefighter named Leon Smith drove Ladder Company 118 that day across the span. Leon and all five of his company perished at Ground Zero. I was privileged to attend his funeral service and a brother firefighter said of Leon that day, "You were never afraid of fighting a fire with Leon because the fire was afraid of him." I would entitle that picture of their fire truck upon the Brooklyn Bridge "Bridge to Eternity." As they sought to save people from the physical fire, they unknowingly were moments from eternity in either heaven or hell. Do urban firefighters have a greater passion to pull lives from earthly fires than we Bible-believing Christians have to compassionately seek the salvation of souls from eternal fire? Jude 22-23 relates our responsibility to risk our lives in seeking souls: "And of some have compassion, making a difference: and others save with fear, pulling them out of the fire; hating even the garment spotted by the flesh." We can take the "Fireman's Prayer" to heart as a prayer that shows a willingness to make sacrifices for others:

When I am called to duty, God, whenever the flames may rage,

Give me strength to save some life, whatever be its age.

Help me embrace a little child before it is too late,

Or save an older person from the horror of that fate.

Enable me to be alert and hear the weakest shout,

And quickly and efficiently to put the fire out.

I want to fill my calling, and to give the best in me,

To guard my every neighbor and protect his property.

And if, according to my fate, I am to lose my life,

Please bless with your protecting hand my Family, Friends, and Wife.

BOLDNESS FOR ROME

"For I am not ashamed of the gospel of Christ: for it is the power of God unto salvation to every one that believeth; to the Jew first, and also to the Greek" (Romans 1:16). Paul boldly declared his desire to bring the gospel to the capital of the world. He believed His gospel could break into the hearts of both Jews and Gentiles. The primary need of all people, Jew or Gentile, will ever be the gospel of Christ. We must preach without favoritism of a person's culture. This gospel reveals the righteousness of God and makes a man righteous before God.

In a city of *military power,* Paul was bold to proclaim a greater power. Rome displayed the power of man, but the gospel of Christ is the power of God unto salvation. To the Roman mind, war and triumph were important concepts of human happiness. Paul understood that the sacrificial death of Christ and His great resurrection can conquer the soul, change us completely, and make us "more than conquerors through him that loved us" (Romans 8:37). Rome may have been the conquering power of the world, but the gospel of Christ was the conquering power of Rome. Paul believed that the powerful gospel of Christ could conquer Rome.

In a city of great *moral wickedness,* Paul boldly declared that the gospel of Christ has far greater power than the sin in the city. Sometimes the word "power" is translated "miracles" in the New Testament (I Corinthians 12:29). When one believes in Christ, it is a miracle to see such a one changed from the inside out and delivered from the penalty and power of sin! "For with the heart man believeth unto righteousness; and with the mouth confession is made unto salvation" (Romans 10:10). Paul believed that the powerful gospel of Christ could result in the forgiveness of any sin.

In a city of *human intellect,* Paul was bold to say that he was not ashamed to proclaim the gospel of Christ, which can conquer men who deem themselves to be wise. He was not ashamed to challenge humanistic philosophies that challenge the gospel message. He was not ashamed to say that there was only one way to heaven. He was not ashamed to say in Rome, "The wages of sin is death, but the gift of God is eternal life through Jesus Christ our Lord" (Romans 6:23). Paul believed that the powerful gospel of Christ could make a foolish man wise.

In a city of *empty religion,* paganism, and man-made tradition, Paul knew he preached the true power of God unto salvation, for the gospel can save those who are trapped in the error of false religion. "For therein is the righteousness of God revealed from faith to faith: as it is written, The just shall live by faith" (Romans 1:17). Paul laid bare the theme of this mighty book: to demonstrate that salvation is by the righteousness of Jesus Christ imputed to the believing sinner. Paul believed that the powerful gospel of Christ alone revealed the righteousness of God and could save the ungodly no matter what religion they professed.

One day I looked out on Flatbush Avenue and saw three teenage boys throwing apples and oranges at the fruit market across the street from our church. I decided to go out to try to talk to the young men. They were having a great time as I approached them. I went to the smallest of the three teens and lightly touched his arm. "Come on, why are you throwing that fruit at the hard working people in the fruit market?" I said. Once I touched him, he jumped nearly into my face and he angrily screamed, "Don't touch me, get out of my face!" Then he took a few steps back, threw the last piece of fruit at me, and hit me in the face! After a few more minutes, they began to walk away from me, and I preached to them as they departed. "You must come to Jesus Christ and be born again, or you will die and go to hell." Just a couple of days later, I walked across Flatbush Avenue to a pharmacy. There was a light, drizzling rain. In front of the pharmacy was a bus stop, and my three friends were there waiting for a bus. Our eyes met, and although a wave of fear passed through me, I did not want to show them that fear, so I approached them. As the small guy was cutting his fingernails with a carpet knife, he curled his lips and said bitterly, "You know, when it rains like this, I just feel like cutting people up." I asked him his name. "Homicide," he answered. I asked the medium-sized teen his name. "Suicide," he said coldly. I asked the third fellow his name. He was the tallest of the three. "Jerome," he said. At least one of them was being honest with me. Then Jerome looked down at me and asked a serious question. "Why are you talking to us?" I answered, "Because you need Jesus Christ as your Savior." Jerome responded, "Man, you're bold!" That is my desire as God gives me breath to speak. Often I am not as bold as I should be. I lack courage at times just like anyone else, but my desire is to speak boldly the gospel of Jesus Christ.

Yes, the gospel was more powerful than Rome's pagan religions, Rome's mighty military, Rome's proud intellectuals, Rome's violent mobs, and Rome's deep wickedness! Paul unashamedly proclaimed this gospel of grace in the great cities of his day and so must we. The gospel of Christ remains as powerful today as ever, and we must believe that the God of the gospel can do the miracle of salvation in the hearts of Jews and Gentiles in our present generation. As we begin to behold the city, we must look with the right attitude! Is your attitude one of thankfulness, homesickness, indebtedness, readiness, and boldness to reach our mighty metropolitan areas for Christ?

CHAPTER 2

The City Has Not Changed

Everyone likes to go sightseeing. We have had many visitors and youth groups visit us in "The Big Apple" through the years, and I have not found one person yet who did not enjoy seeing the famous city sights. New York City is famous for its sights—the Statue of Liberty, the Empire State Building, and Rockefeller Center. New York City has it all! If I could, I would take you to a sight that is not very well known; at this sight we can go "soul-seeing." Imagine yourself standing on the top of the Kosciuszko Bridge. This bridge, a part of the Brooklyn-Queens Expressway, joins Brooklyn and Queens. First you face west, looking at the awesome Manhattan skyline. Then, you look to your left to view the two and a half million people of Brooklyn. To your right sits the borough of Queens, which is home for two million people. Again you turn toward Manhattan. The incredible skyline represents the home for one and a half million people and place of employment for another million and a half souls. As you stand atop this bridge, you can easily imagine the living souls of New York City. But now I want you to look down. As you focus your eyes below, a huge graveyard that seems to have no end comes into sight. It seems the immense cemetery does not end until you see the Empire State Building and Chrysler Building rise with human might into the sky. This is the sight that stirs my soul. It is a sight of the living and the dead. It reminds me that no matter how much success or wealth, sadness or poverty one has in this world, we all must live somewhere forever. No matter how tall man's buildings rise, they still fall short of heaven. It reminds me that in a very real way, the city has not changed. The city is still a gathering place of people. People are made in the image of God but have fallen from that image and now live separated from Him if they do not believe in His Son, Jesus Christ.

I am fascinated with the city. I love to study what the Bible says about the city, and I love to live and preach the gospel to the city. The theme of the city leaps from the pages of Scripture as I read the Word of God. The word "city" appears 870 times in 779 Bible verses. The word "cities" appears 448 times in 394 verses. This theme begins in Genesis with the cities of man and ends in Revelation with the eternal city of God. Jesus presently builds this eternal city of glory for us. The Bible is a book about the city! A number of Bible books contain strong urban themes. Jonah and Nahum center on the city of Nineveh. Lamentations reveals Jeremiah's broken heart for the city of Jerusalem. Ezra and Nehemiah focus on rebuilding the temple and walls of Jerusalem. Micah writes about the capital cities, Samaria and Jerusalem. The Acts of the Apostles tells how the gospel broke into key population centers in the first century. Many of the epistles were written to those important cities of the first century world: Romans, I and II Corinthians, Ephesians, Philippians, and I and II Thessalonians. First and II Timothy were written to the young man of God pastoring in the large city of Ephesus. John addresses the Book of Revelation to seven churches in key cities of Asia Minor. Yes, the Bible is a book about the city! Let's go back in time to some of the first cities mentioned in the Bible and do a little sightseeing of souls in the Scripture.

SOULS STILL COME TO THE CITY

In the first appearance of the word "city" in our Bible, we see that "Cain went out from the presence of the Lord and . . . builded a city"

(Genesis 4:16-17). Many things could be said about this passage of Scripture, but here is what I would like you to see: the reason Cain went to establish this first city is the same reason souls come to the city today.

Ever since Cain, the city has drawn people to it. It has a spellbinding magnetism. What a sight to see, a soul who has committed a terrible *crime*. Can you see Cain strike his brother dead and leave him in a pool of blood? "And Cain talked with Abel his brother: and it came to pass, when they were in the field, that Cain rose up against Abel his brother, and slew him" (Genesis 4:8). Cain commits this violent act against his brother out of anger toward God. When a man is angry against God, he takes out his anger on man. Because of Cain's sin, God places him under a well-deserved but awful *curse*. This curse leads Cain to a life of struggling and shifting. "And now art thou cursed from the earth, which hath opened her mouth to receive thy brother's blood from thy hand; when thou tillest the ground, it shall not henceforth yield unto thee her strength; a fugitive and a vagabond shalt thou be in the earth" (Genesis 4:11-12). Cain now lives a life of instability. Next we see Cain echo a selfish and fearful *complaint*. "And Cain said unto the Lord, My punishment is greater than I can bear. Behold, thou hast driven me out this day from the face of the earth; and from thy face shall I be hid; and I shall be a fugitive and a vagabond in the earth; and it shall come to pass, that every one that findeth me shall slay me" (Genesis 4:13-14). Cain sounds like the rich fool in his inward focus (Luke 12:13-21). He sounds like a spoiled child who did not get his way. He is the father of those who live by the motto "Life is not fair!" Cain fears that his murder of Abel will lead to revenge and eventually his own death.

What did Cain need? He needed security. What did Cain do? He built a city. The city was a way for Cain to live a little easier while he was under the curse God placed upon him. By building this city, he hoped to overcome the curse of struggle and shifting in his own human strength. The city was his way of dealing with the curse without God. Cain sought for a measure of security and protection in his life under a curse. Cain called the city "'Enoch' which means 'initiation' or 'dedication.' Cain dedicates a new world" separated from God.[1] Roger Greenway writes in *Cities: Missions' New Frontier* that "Cain built a city, for urban life structures and protects human life."[2] Even though violence and strife are a part of city life, "the cities that fallen humans build are 'common grace' cities, made possible only by God's mercy to all mankind."[3]

People still come to the city. They have committed acts of sin and are living under the curse of sin. "For there is no difference: for all have sinned, and come short of the glory of God" (Romans 3:22*b*-23). Sin still leads to chaotic, unstable living. "A man shall not be established by wickedness: but the root of the righteous shall not be moved" (Proverbs 12:3). By nature man is fearful and seeks to find a measure of security while under the curse. The way of Cain is alive and well, and his bloodstained hands have not departed from the city. His heartless lies and attitude thrive in the city today. His wandering and struggling typify many in our cities today. People today are drawn to the city seeking for the same thing Cain sought in the first city ever built. People are looking for security in the midst of their instability. What most do not realize, however, is that what they truly seek cannot be found in the city.

People come expecting to find security but find *disregard* for God and His ways. "And Cain went out from the presence of the Lord . . . and he builded a city" (Genesis 4:16-17). Cain typifies the common man who puts his own agenda ahead of God's will. Cain walked away from the one true God, whom he considered unreasonable, and reasoned that he would do it his way. Although no man can flee from God's presence (Psalm 139:7-8), sinful man can seek to satisfy his own dreams without consulting his Creator.

People come to cities hoping to find peace and prosperity, but they often find *disorder*. Cain's urban civilization led to moral and spiritual chaos. The first attack upon the institution of marriage occured in

Cain's city. "And Lamech took unto him two wives: the name of the one was Adah, and the name of the other Zillah" (Genesis 4:19). This war against God's plan of marriage between one man and one woman rages today. The city remains the place where deviant sexuality still finds acceptance. Cities continue to be center stage in the promotion of lifestyles and values that attack the family order instituted by God.

In spite of Cain's disregard for God and the disorder to which it led, Cain's city made great *discoveries*. There was marketing and free enterprise. "And Adah bare Jabal: he was the father of such as dwell in tents, and of such as have cattle" (Genesis 4:20). It was a hot spot for music, entertainment, and pleasure. "And his brother's name was Jubal: he was the father of all such as handle the harp and organ" (Genesis 4:21). It was a center of industry and metallurgy. "And Zillah, she also bare Tubal-cain, an instructer of every artificer in brass and iron" (Genesis 4:22). There was violence and culture, industry and pleasure, marketing and music, side by side!

The city has not changed. Cities today still attract multitudes through employment, entertainment, and educational opportunities. Cities provide great job opportunities for people with or without education. The common laborer or the world-class doctor or entertainer can find work in a large city. I remember the millennium celebrations that occurred around the world on the night of December 31, 1999, which brought in the year 2000. In every nation, the key city was the center of excitement. The alluring nightlife of clubs, discos, and all-night parties attracts multitudes of searching and sinful souls. New York City, Boston, and other major American urban areas draw the world's best and brightest intellects to major universities and hospitals for advanced learning.

People still come to major cities seeking for a security that the city cannot ultimately provide. They come to New York City from Africa, Europe, Russia, Asia, the West Indies, South America, and nearly every other nation on earth. The world has come to us in the city! We have a tremendous opportunity to get the gospel to all the colors and cultures of the world right here in our own nation. Many come to our American cities from places we cannot go with the gospel. Souls seek for security, and we have the real answer: Jesus Christ.

Our first ministry in New York City was in the Flatbush area in the center of Brooklyn. This is a West Indian community with many first generation immigrants. Many come to make a better life, leaving behind family, children, and loved ones. Sometimes they find this better life. Sometimes the better life eludes them. They come to New York City looking for security; many find only chaos. The ones with real joy realize that true security comes only through Jesus Christ. Unless people seek the Lord, the Devil tears away at them, destroying them from the inside out.

I have often seen the city rip away at the inner man, eventually destroying the outer man. I remember a young man from Africa named Marbu. He professed faith in Christ while living in Africa, but he drifted from his commitment to follow Jesus. He was in Brooklyn without proper immigration papers, driving a taxi during the night without a driver license or registration, getting robbed, and living in a one room apartment. Frustration and instability filled his life. Nevertheless, he stayed, hoping to find security in this world under the curse of sin. He still saw the city as his best hope although the city had ripped out of his heart the desire he once had to seek the Lord.

I remember a tough guy named Ricardo from Panama. Ricardo spoke with a raspy voice and called me "Father." I would say kindly to him, "Ricardo, you do not have to call me Father. Call me Pastor!" He would say, "OK, Father." He lived out on the street. I talked to him about Jesus, and he even prayed to receive the Lord, but I did not see any changes in his life. One time he stole twenty-five chairs from our church and pawned them. Another time we let him use our shower because he was so dirty, and later I realized that during his shower he had stolen our hair clippers from the bathroom! Honesty and integrity had been ripped out of Ricardo, and deceit and guile had become his life.

I visited Locksley, who lived in a Bronx project. Locksley came from a Christian home in Jamaica looking for a better life, but he developed into a slave to crack. Crack vials littered the elevator up to his apartment. He destroyed himself with the drugs he poured into his body. His live-in girlfriend delivered one of their babies in the bathroom of their project apartment. She feared going to a city hospital, thinking that a city agency would remove their children from their care. She was right. After the baby was delivered, they had to go to the hospital. When the physicians discovered drugs in her system, the city put their other three children into the foster care system.

Many people come to the city as believers in Jesus Christ. If they do not find a strong church, the sin and temptation of the city brings devastation. I knew a brilliant medical doctor named Dennis. Dennis came to Christ in his home in St. Vincent, but he did not live for Christ in the city. He contracted HIV and infected a number of women through his immorality before he died. I preached his funeral; three women were present whom he had infected with that virus. As we went to the graveside to lay Dennis's body to rest, one of the women who was very sick with that deadly virus just looked into the grave where his casket lay. She stood there and cried after everyone else had left. She knew that she would be in a casket in the same ground in a short amount of time. The thought of living with dying while trying to raise three small children was overwhelming to her. I went over to comfort her as she peered down at Dennis's casket in the ground. I told her that the grace of Jesus Christ saves a person from sin, death, and hell. I prayed with her to see the Lord.

Once while I distributed tracts on the streets of Manhattan, a sign caught my eye. Outside a large concrete structure I read "Big Apple Wrecking and Construction Corp." Inside this building, a huge crane ripped away, tearing away and dismantling the entire building. It was the Paladium, a well-known concert center and nightclub.

Eventually the outside would also be torn down, but they ripped out the inside first. The Devil works to destroy lives in the same way. He rips away at the heart and soul of a person, removing faith, hope, and love. Bit by bit, the city, like that crane, can tear away at a person's faith until the outer man eventually crumbles as well. As I looked at that building being torn down from the inside out, I thought of Marbu, Ricardo, Dennis, and Locksley.

Others come to the city and realize the only security that matters resides in the love of Jesus Christ. Church turns into a haven for them! Chris came to New York City from Saint Lucia and immediately attended our church. God's blessing upon his life evidenced itself in countless ways. This young man actively involved himself in our church, leading the singing, teaching Sunday school, and going out on church visitation. He met a fine Christian girl and got married. He worked for a realtor and eventually obtained his own real estate license. We saw a number of believers come from a church in Barbados, which had been started by a Gospel Fellowship Association missionary years ago. Our church provided a place for them to continue in their Christian faith. Charles and Tammy walked into our church one Sunday morning. He lived with Tammy for eight years before getting married. He had tried the Muslim faith, the Hindu faith, and other religions as well. Someone invited him to our church. After they visited a few times, I went over to their home and we began having Bible studies. They grew as they soaked in the Word of God. Yes, some realize that the security they really need is the security found in Jesus Christ!

SATAN STILL CONTROLS THE CITY

In Babel we see a city and society established by Nimrod under the power and control of Satan. Babel, later known as Babylon (Genesis 10:10), was the center of Nimrod's civilization. Nimrod's kingdom not only still exists but it still dominates the desires of depraved men. Up to this moment the Devil has not relinquished this control.

BEHOLD THE CITY

After the Flood, God had told Noah to "be fruitful, and multiply, and replenish the earth" (Genesis 9:1). Nimrod and the people of Babel, however, rebelled against God's clear mandate. They sought to build "a city and a tower . . . lest we be scattered abroad upon the face of the whole earth" (Genesis 11:4). These desires collided with God's command.

Satan, the god of this world and the prince of the power of the air, seeks to make the city his stronghold, and he was the mastermind behind this mighty man Nimrod. Nimrod means "Let us rebel."[4] In Genesis 10:8-9 we read, "And Cush begat Nimrod: he began to be a mighty one in the earth. He was a mighty hunter before the Lord: wherefore it is said, Even as Nimrod the mighty hunter before the Lord." This mighty hunter did not hunt for deer or quail, but he sought to capture the souls of men. He lived before the Lord, which means that he knew God saw him and knew him, but he did not submit to Him. Nimrod lived in defiance of God's Word. He sought to deceive men to follow the ungodly goals that he valued and the false religion that he established. The paganism, idolatry, and spiritism originating in Babel eventually filtered around the globe. These religions still prosper today; Nimrod's spirit of rebellion flourishes seemingly as never before. No where do they succeed more than in the major cities of our world. "In cities the fiercest battles for human minds and hearts take place. For that reason, cities are center stage for the Christian mission, the great drama of redemption."[5] Yes, Satan controlled the mind and heart of Nimrod as this marksman lived in violent resistance to God, hunting for the souls of men to corrupt and plunder.

The foundation for Babel was human pride and ambition. These are Satan's delights. Genesis 11:1-9 describes the planting of the city of Babel and God's displeasure with the builders' haughty behavior. "And they said one to another, Go to, let us make brick, and burn them thoroughly. And they had brick for stone, and slime had they for morter. And they said, Go to, let us build us a city and a tower, whose top may reach unto heaven; and let us make us a name, lest we be scattered abroad upon the face of the whole earth" (Genesis 11:3-4). This tower, the first "skyscraper" we find in biblical history, was the centerpiece for Nimrod's false religion of paganism and idolatry. The tower would make men stand in awe. Many skyscrapers are still built on the foundation of human pride. This building would be the cultural and religious center of the kingdom, and it would be a symbol of human unity and strength. It stood for man's "success" apart from a loving God, who gave him the strength to build it in the first place. The structure would attract men to Nimrod's selfish city. The flood had not changed man's heart, and the "way of Cain" was still present in Babel (Jude 11). God's response to their desire is clear. "This they begin to do: and now nothing will be restrained from them, which they have imagined to do." God did not approve of their building plans so he confused their language.

Babylon in the Bible is more than a city; it is a world system of which Satan is prince. Satan himself is precisely described in Isaiah 14:12-14 as one full of pride. Satan's system still has not been destroyed. The lust of the flesh, the lust of the eyes, and the pride of life (I John 2:15-17) still ruin many while making huge amounts of money for others. The actual city of Babylon has been demolished, but the spirit of Babylon thrives today. This world system will be destroyed only before the coming of Christ.

Revelation 18:2-3 tells of the corrupting influence of the ungodly city first established by Nimrod. "Babylon the great is fallen, is fallen, and is become the habitation of devils, and the hold of every foul spirit, and a cage of every unclean and hateful bird. For all nations have drunk of the wine of the wrath of her fornication, and the kings of the earth have committed fornication with her, and the merchants of the earth are waxed rich through the abundance of her delicacies." Babylon is a city fully corrupt spiritually, morally, and economically. From the very beginning, the city of Babylon was Satan's stronghold.

The church of Jesus Christ must not retreat from this battleground. The gates of hell, which the church ought to attack, will not prevail against God's Spirit-filled church (Matthew 16:18). People must realize when they minister for Jesus Christ in a great city that they are entering Satan's stronghold. Pastor Jerry Walker, a friend of mine who has ministered for many years in Brooklyn, said once, "The city is not merely the Devil's backyard; it is the Devil's living room!" We are in a spiritual battle, and the heart of this battle is in the city. Satan seeks to deceive and destroy the heart of man from the God who sent His Son to save them. Satan dupes through false religions. The city is a place of intense spiritual warfare, and false religions still abound and appear to have much success in the city. Ever since Nimrod, cities have been centers of religion. In the days of Paul, Antioch was filled with gross immorality, Athens was filled with idols, and Ephesus proudly worshiped the goddess Diana. Things are no different today. From the cold ceremonies of the Roman Catholic Church to the deadness of theological liberalism to the deceptions of the cults, cities are still centers of false religion.

Nevertheless, we are not called to retreat from the city but to reach our cities! The city has not changed, but neither has the power of the gospel we preach. The Lord taught us that the world will hate us and that we live in the world without being of the world (John 15:18-19; 17:14-18). God has not called His church to monastic living but to missionary giving. Jesus sends us into the world. As "strangers and pilgrims" we must deny fleshly lusts, "which war against the soul," in order to have an honest walk among those under the power of the world system (I Peter 2:11). We must bring the gospel to those deceived by temporal materialism and false religion. Jesus Christ gives us the power to hold forth the word of life even in "a crooked and perverse" culture. God says we have His grace, the desire and power to do His will, to shine, not in our holy huddles but even in the midst of urban crookedness and darkness (Philippians 2:15-16).

SIN STILL CONDEMNS THE CITY

Let us now go to a third awesome city sight. Here we see a group of cities burning down, the smoke rising up "as the smoke of a furnace" (Genesis 19:28). The cities are Sodom, Gomorrah, Admah, and Zeboim (Deuteronomy 29:23). When people think of cities in the Bible, this passage in Genesis usually comes to the mind. Some might falsely conclude from this narrative that the spiritual decision for any believer is to avoid the city. Many wrongly determine that the city is no place for a Christian to live, for Lot pitched his tent toward Sodom, was drawn into it, became lukewarm in it, and barely escaped it. Lot lost much in the city. His wife looked back at Sodom with longing eyes and became a pillar of salt. His sons-in-law remained in the city and perished. His daughters later got him drunk and conceived children that would be enemies to the nation of Israel. Should we conclude from this that a follower of Christ should avoid the city? Does Lot's way have to be the experience of all God's people who live in the city?

The sins and wickedness of Sodom, Gomorrah, and the cities on that plain came up before God. These cities that had given "themselves over to fornication, and going after strange flesh, are set forth for an example, suffering the vengeance of eternal fire" (Jude 7). Ezekiel describes Sodom's sin as "pride, fulness of bread, and abundance of idleness . . . neither did she strengthen the hand of the poor and needy" (16:49). The scene depicted in God's Word demonstrates the utter depravity of the people. The men of the city gathered together to violently rape the angelic visitors. Lot's alarming lack of courage and total loss of perspective led him to offer his daughters to the morally perverted men pounding on his door. Henry Morris properly concludes that the sins of the inhabitants of Sodom and Gomorrah and "this descent into degeneracy, is caused first of all by a rejection of God as Creator and Sovereign."[6]

The humanistic and evolutionary culture of America is slipping quickly into the moral perversions and proud idleness that caused

God to destroy Sodom and Gomorrah. Our church in Manhattan initially met at a YMCA building in the Chelsea area. This community is a thriving gay and lesbian community where many are saturated with the lie that homosexuals are "born that way." What we are born with is a deceitful and desperately wicked heart. We easily are deceived into believing lies.

While I was distributing tracts one night, a teenage girl walking past me brazenly asked, "Can I have a tract even though I am Satan?" "Of course," I said. She asked if I approved of the homosexual lifestyle. I told her that God does not, and I take my stand with the God of the Bible. This young girl then announced her love for another teenage girl who accompanied her. These kinds of encounters break my heart, for I know they caused God to pour down his judgment upon civilizations.

Christians ought to move to the city, but for the right reason. If the nightlife and bright lights of the city allure the child of God, he must stay far away from urban life. If the lust for power, possessions, or pleasure draws one to the city, then that one should not live in the city. Lot was drawn to the city of Sodom for the wrong reasons, and soon he "sat in the gate of Sodom" (Genesis 19:1). He focused on gaining social standing in the city rather than being a spiritual influence. Rather than seek to proclaim the name of God in Sodom, Lot contented himself with sitting at the gate. This is such a sad sight! There Lot discussed business, made decisions, transacted trade, or simply spoke about issues of importance in the city. He, however, had no influence among the people for righteousness. He failed to share the goodness and mercy of God with the inhabitants of Sodom. He could have showed them how God had demonstrated His grace earlier by delivering them from the kings of the east. He also could have reminded them of the powerful testimony of the King-Priest Melchizedek (Genesis 14).

The sins of the city wore down the already carnal Lot spiritually and emotionally. Lot shows us the difficulties and dangers of a saved man in a sinful city. He was a man "just" and "righteous" in God's sight (II Peter 2:7-8), but he was spiritually blind to his accommodation of the sins all around him. Living in Sodom, "in seeing and hearing, vexed his righteous soul from day to day with their unlawful deeds" (II Peter 2:8). The worldliness slowly infiltrated his thinking to the point that he was willing to keep peace with those Sodomites by surrendering his two virgin daughters for the satisfaction of their lust. Perhaps Lot feared that his business ventures would fail or his status in their sight would be lowered if he did not cave in to their obsessive demands. His lukewarmness spewed out of his hypocritical heart as he warned his sons-in-law of the judgment to come. The Scripture indicts not the content of his message but the tone: "he seemed as one that mocked" (Genesis 19:14). The word "mocked" is translated "play" in Exodus 32:6, when the nation of Israel worshiped the golden calf as they "sat down to eat and to drink, and rose up to play." His witness was worthless; his passivity was evident when Lot lingered in his escape from the city. It is as if he did not believe the very message that he playfully proclaimed.

There are two reasons one goes to the city. One may go as Lot, lured with the sins of the city. The list of enticing sins that may lead a person to inhabit a city is endless. The city does not need any more mocking missionaries and passive preachers who do not speak with the conviction that leads others to believe in the one true God. Lot was a mocking missionary. The people of Sodom did not need any more believers sitting at the gate doing business without concern for the spiritual destiny of their eternal souls. Sodom already had one too many careless believers. Such believers in God do not lead sinners to salvation and do not keep back a city from destruction. On the other hand, one may enter into the city as a Nehemiah, burdened for the broken walls and with a desire to see them restored. One may go forth into cities full of sin and ripe for judgment and be as Paul, who "so spake, that a great multitude both of the Jews and also of the Greeks believed" (Acts 14:1). As Christians move to the city, they must witness in the city. The city always needs more godly people proclaiming the name of the Lord and His salvation.

As we ponder these early cities in the Bible, we learn that the essence of the human city has not changed. The sights of these cities should stir our soul to the need that gets larger with the daily increase of urban population. Just as Cain went to the city seeking security, people from all cultures still come to the city. Just as Nimrod led others to rebel against God in his city, so Satan seeks to deceive and control the hearts and minds of people in the city. Unlike Lot, who carelessly sat at the city gate while his city was on the brink of judgment, we must not neglect our responsibility to speak boldly for our God while we live in great urban areas.

We see that God brings His righteous judgment upon the cities of men. A worldwide flood destroyed Cain's city. The confusion of languages was an evidence of judgment upon Babel. Fire ravaged Sodom and Gomorrah. Throughout Scripture and human history, the cities of men have turned to rubble. Cities, being the fountainheads of sin, become the focus of His wrath. The souls in the city today need to see that the only city that will last forever is the eternal city of God. The wages of sin is ever death, and urban inhabitants need the gospel before judgment overtakes their soul. Will you pray about going to the city not merely to see sights but to seek souls?

---

[1]Jacques Ellul, *The Meaning of the City* (Carlisle, U.K.: Great Britain Paternoster Press, 1997), p. 5.

[2]Roger S. Greenway and Timothy M. Monsma, *Cities: Missions' New Frontier* (Grand Rapids: Baker Book House, 2000), p. 28.

[3]Greenway, p. 29.

[4]Henry Morris, *The Genesis Record* (Grand Rapids: Baker Book House, 1976), p. 251.

[5]Greenway, p. 31.

[6]Morris, p. 348.

CHAPTER 3

A Psalm for the City

As we started Parkway Baptist Church in Queens, I moved pews out of a U-Haul truck into the storefront building we were renting. It was Saturday, 9:00 P.M. A big guy named Gregory spied an opening to make some easy money by helping to unload the truck, so he asked if he could help move the pews into the church for "only" fifteen dollars. I bargained him down to ten dollars. He carried the pews by himself without much effort. I slipped him ten dollars and turned around to find a gospel tract to give him. He had disappeared into the night. He got all he thought he needed. A couple of days later someone asked me if I had heard about the shooting on the block that same Saturday night. I said no and asked who had been shot. It was Gregory. He got shot in the head, but he survived. Miraculously, God spared his life. I visited Gregory in the hospital, and he had a large scar on his head that was in the shape of a perfect question mark. As I spoke to him, I knew that God had spared his life by a fraction of an inch. At a loss for words, I said, "Gregory, God put a question mark in your head! He must be asking you a question: what will you do with your life? What will you do with Jesus?"

I will never forget his sad response: "Crack, crack, crack. I would hustle and steal just to do a little crack. I won't do crack anymore, but I'll never give up marijuana or beer. There is nothing wrong with those things."

When released from the hospital, Gregory returned to the streets. Soon he knocked at our church door, conning me for more money in order to buy drugs or alcohol. He told me that his car had broken down and he needed money to have it towed. With alcohol on his breath and bloodshot eyes, he pleaded with me to give him some money. He told me forcefully and with desperation, "Come on, Rev, we go back!" I was not sure what we went back to, but I stood firm and refused to give him any money. I never saw him again. Gregory reminds me of the violence and guile that David saw in the city streets of his day.

HOW DO YOU FEEL IN THE CITY?

Have you ever wanted to run? This is a common desire for urban dwellers. King David wrote Psalm 55 from the city of Jerusalem and describes *how he felt* in response to two things. His son Absalom had rebelled against him and led a coup d'état. Then David's trusted counselor, Ahithophel, betrayed him and took sides with Absalom in the insurrection. David refers to his traitorous friend Ahithophel in Psalm 55:12-13: "For it was not an enemy that reproached me; then I could have borne it . . . but it was thou, a man mine equal, my guide, and mine acquaintance." Because of the treachery of these two close associations of David, the terror of death gripped his soul. The city of Jerusalem, the beloved city of God, became a place that David longed to flee. The "voice of the enemy" (Psalm 55:3) overpowered the voice of those who desired righteousness. Violence prevailed in Jerusalem; loneliness and fear dominated David's heart. Trembling overtook his body. David laments, "Oh that I had wings like a dove! for then would I fly away, and be at rest" (Psalm 55:6). In reading the account of Absalom's rebellion in II Samuel 15, it seems strange that David had so quickly and easily abdicated his earthly power. David offered no resistance to maintain his throne. "And there came a messenger to

David, saying, The hearts of the men of Israel are after Absalom. And David said unto all his servants that were with him at Jerusalem, Arise, and let us flee; for we shall not else escape from Absalom: make speed to depart, lest he overtake us suddenly, and bring evil upon us, and smite the city with the edge of the sword" (II Samuel 15:13-14). David lost his love for the city of God, and all desire for earthly power disappeared; the fear of death fell upon his soul.

WHAT DO YOU SEE IN THE CITY?

Next David describes *what he saw in the city* (Psalm 55:9-11). David personifies the wicked activity in the city. He tells of seven different kinds of devious people who wandered the city streets. He speaks of Mr. Violence and Mr. Strife guarding the city with their crime and their conflict. Cruelty, oppression, and constant contention swirled around the sad streets. David saw Mr. Mischief and Mr. Sorrow in the midst of the city, working their confusion, frustration, and hopelessness. The word "sorrow" speaks of miserable labor that does not satisfy but results in pain. Mr. Wickedness stood alone in the city. This word refers to disaster that leads to destruction. He is like the speeding driver who is an accident waiting to happen! Not even Mr. Violence or Mr. Strife could trust him. Finally, David saw Mr. Deceit and Mr. Guile throughout the city streets. Deceitful men cut others to pieces in order to get ahead. They work deception and treachery leading to betrayal.

Cities take on the character of their citizens. Jerusalem is often called a city of truth and a holy city (Zechariah 8:3; Isaiah 48:2; 52:1). A city can also be identified by joy (Jeremiah 49:25; Acts 8:8). Cities also can be proud (Zephaniah 2:15), oppressive (Zephaniah 3:1), and violent (Nahum 3:1). Cities experience the blessing of God and the curse of God (Deuteronomy 28:3, 16).[1] As David wrote Psalm 55, the joy of the city of Jerusalem had departed and the violent aspect of urban life had risen like a mighty tidal wave.

Living in the city, one cannot miss seeing the violence and strife first-hand. While living on Flatbush Avenue in Brooklyn, I woke up one morning to find an abandoned car riddled with bullet holes crashed into the storefront across the street from our church. One evening I went into a city project building to pick up a family for church. As I approached the tenement, drug dealers surrounded me. They thought I was their supplier. They encircled me and with eyes of anticipation looked intently at me, expecting something from me. I told them, "I am a preacher. Here is what I have for you." I gave them gospel tracts! Were they ever surprised, for they were expecting drugs! Another day I opened up the newspaper to find the picture of a young girl who had attended our vacation Bible school. She was killed while walking through the lobby of her apartment building; she was in the wrong place at the wrong time and became tragically caught in the crossfire of a drug war. Another young lady named Anita who attended our Bible clubs for a number of years was killed in what became known as "The Wendy's Massacre." Two thugs broke into a Wendy's near closing time and bound and gagged Anita along with her six coworkers. Anita and four others were killed. Two young men miraculously escaped death. Thirty-six hours after the crime, John and Craig were arrested. The crime left such a bloody memory on the community that the Wendy's was razed to the ground and a new store was built. I can relate to David when he said, "I have seen violence and strife in the city. Day and night they go about it upon the walls thereof: mischief and sorrow are in the midst of it" (Psalm 55:9-10).

My philosophy in dealing with the violence in our city is to stay out of the wrong places at the wrong times. I have frequented dangerous city streets in daylight hours, but I am convinced that a majority of the crime takes place in the middle of the night when I sleep. One ultimately must simply trust God and rest in the promise that "the steps of a good man are ordered by the Lord: and he delighteth in his way" (Psalm 37:23). God Himself delights in the pathway of His redeemed.

One day, I offered a drug dealer a gospel tract and he snarled back, "I am on another boat." I replied, "Is your boat going to sink?" He did not like my words. He retorted, "Beat it and do your preaching down on Ditmas [the next block]. This corner is hot."

I shook the dust off my feet and walked away. Not long after that incident a young police officer was gunned down in the middle of the night by a drug dealer on that same block.

Daily life, no matter where you live, carries danger. While on deputation, Debbie and I drove along a lonely two-lane Kansas road. Debbie interrupted the boring ride as she shouted at me, "Watch out!" A cow stood in the middle of the road. I quickly swerved out of my lane and barely missed the cow. God graciously allowed no one to be coming in the opposite direction or a head-on collision may have resulted. As Debbie and I went to bed that night, we praised God for His protection. Then the preposterous thought hit me, "What if we hit that cow? The headline of the paper could have read, 'New York City Missionary—Killed by a Cow!'" "I will both lay me down in peace, and sleep for thou, Lord, only makest me dwell in safety" (Psalm 4:8). In this world, the only safe place is the center of God's will.

Many of the victims of crime, although not all—for truly many innocent victims die in our violent culture—are involved with the wrong people in the wrong place at the wrong time. "Thou shalt not follow a multitude to do evil" (Exodus 23:2), for happy and content is the man who doesn't walk with the ungodly, stand with the sinners, or sit with the scorners.

WHO MUST WE TRUST IN THE CITY?

In the midst of David's fear, Psalm 55:12-23 shows *whom he trusted in the city.* David trusted in God. Here we see a believer crying to God from the city, calling out to God and pouring out his soul in the midst of his loneliness and fear, "Give ear to my prayer, O God; and hide not thyself from my supplication" (Psalm 55:1). If we could see within the walls of the millions of homes and apartments throughout our great cities, we would see souls crying out to God. In the midst of the violence, there are souls who cry, "Attend unto me, and hear me" (Psalm 55:2*a*). The cry of David went up three times a day to the Lord. "As for me, I will call upon God; and the Lord shall save me. Evening, and morning, and at noon, will I pray, and cry aloud: and he shall hear my voice" (Psalm 55:16-17).

To live for God in the city requires prayer. Like David, we ought to set our watch to pray three times a day because many temptations harass a child of God in the city. It has been a privilege to pastor many people through the years who know how to pray: women who pray with tender tears coursing down their cheeks, wives who pray for their husbands and children, and men who cry out to God for His mercy and grace to help in time of need. One of my main goals as an urban pastor is to have a church that prays to our heavenly Father in the name of the Lord Jesus Christ in the power of the Holy Spirit. "For through Him we both have access by one Spirit unto the Father" (Ephesians 2:18). Prayer in Jesus' name is our declaration of dependence upon the Lord, and through prayer God delivers and sustains His people. Prayer is agonizing work whereby we recognize our helplessness and God's help.

The Lord Jesus gave us a model prayer that is a masterpiece of wisdom (Matthew 6:9-13). This prayer teaches us that we can pray about any problem; this prayer deals in principle with any life situation. The greatest problem solver known to man is prayer to the Father in the name of Jesus Christ by the power of the Holy Spirit! This prayer was not given by the Lord to be primarily recited from memory in a public worship service. Jesus tells us to pray using this model as a pattern for our private worship.

"Our Father which art in heaven, Hallowed be thy name" answers our search for the truth of God. His eternal *Person* settles the question of God's existence. God is our Maker and Redeemer. Prayer must begin with God's name, not our needs. God is personal ("our Father"), sovereign (He is in heaven), and holy ("hallowed be thy name").

"Thy kingdom come. Thy will be done in earth, as it is in heaven." God has an eternal and earthly *plan* for our life in order to glorify Him. This petition helps us value what God values and make decisions based on what is eternally important: His kingdom and His will.

"Give us this day our daily bread." This request answers all our worries about temporal things. God's *provision* solves our fears. Daily bread, *epiousios* items, can apply to any of the everyday necessities that, though they do not last, are still vital to life: food, clothes, finances, or health.

"And forgive us our debts." Here is God's answer to our sin and guilt. God's *pardon* gives us peace with Him. We need to be forgiven in order to forgive others. Daily forgiveness from God leads to a growing relationship with Him, freedom from guilt, the joy of the Lord, and power for service.

"As we forgive our debtors." This is God's solution to bitterness. We can live in *peace* with our fellow man. Forgiving others is God's antidote to resentment. Forgiveness happens as we face the cross and realize how much God has forgiven us. Forgiveness is not a feeling; forgiveness is not forgetting. Forgiveness is releasing a person from his actions and willingly living with the consequences, realizing God is in control.

"And lead us not into temptation, but deliver us from evil: for thine is the kingdom, and the power, and the glory, for ever. Amen." This is God's comprehensive answer to our fears, trials, and temptations.

God *protects* His children as we focus on His kingdom, rely upon His power, and live for His glory.

My goal is to learn to pray and teach others to pray. The disciples asked the Lord, "Teach us to pray" (Luke 11:1). Amazingly, they never asked Jesus, "Teach us to preach, sing, or prepare sermons!" If we learn to pray, we will have all the fire we need to preach! In our church, we break into prayer groups not only on Wednesday night but also during Sunday morning worship service to beg God for His grace. Sometimes during our Wednesday prayer fellowships we spend nearly the entire service in prayer for various needs: God's glory in our city, the salvation of souls, confession of sin, or missionary needs. "For mine house shall be called an house of prayer for all people" (Isaiah 56:7). Women have weekly prayer partners. We constantly encourage prayer in private, in families, and between husbands and wives. I have been reading Spurgeon's extemporaneous prayers and am praying them myself so that I can learn to pray from men who knew how to pray. Prayer is the only way to make it in a city full of violence and strife. "Therefore I will look unto the Lord; I will wait for the God of my salvation: my God will hear me. Rejoice not against me, O mine enemy: when I fall, I shall arise; when I sit in darkness, the Lord shall be a light unto me" (Micah 7:7-8). God must teach us how to pray if we are going to keep serving Him in dark times or to get up after we fall.

Our phone rang. Edgar and Ana were searching for a church. Their phone call was a definite answer to our prayers for God to draw people to our church. Born in Colombia, South America, Edgar and Ana immigrated to New York City separately and met while in the city. Their lives appeared in excellent order. Their marriage was strong. Edgar had a highly desirable job as a superintendent in the SoHo area of Manhattan. They had two beautiful daughters. Nevertheless, their soul still yearned for the truth that is in Jesus Christ. Raised Roman Catholic, they could not find a church that fed their soul. They visited our church along with their two small daughters. At that time we met in the second floor of a YMCA building, a strange and unimpressive place for Roman Catholics to attend church. On the way out, they asked one of our members if our church was a legitimate ministry. They returned to Heritage Baptist Church, and soon I was sitting at their kitchen table having the first part of a twelve-week Bible study with them about the trustworthiness of Scripture. I did not plan to present the gospel of salvation to them yet, but they possessed such hunger that they literally begged me to show them the way of salvation. At first I hesitated to lead them to the Lord because that was going to be lesson two! I consciously refused to push them into a decision too quickly, but they evidently thirsted for the living water that would spring up "into everlasting life" (John 4:14). I showed them from Scripture what it meant to be saved, we bowed our heads together, and Edgar and Ana believed on the Lord Jesus Christ, trusting His righteousness for their salvation. The following week I still presented the second discipleship lesson on salvation, and I joyfully went through the twelve-week study with them at their kitchen table. Edgar now serves as a deacon in our church, and they serve the Lord in many other ways. In a note Edgar wrote to me at the end of his first year as a believer, he said, "Thank you for all your help during this year. It is great to say that the best thing that happened to us was realizing and accepting Jesus as our Savior. Although the glory is His, you guided us throughout this process." The cities of our world abound with people who are praying to God for direction and truth. We cannot see them, but God does, and as we hold out the lifeline, God can direct our paths to meet.

---

[1]Robert Harris, Gleason Archer, and Bruce Waltke, eds. *Theological Wordbook of the Old Testament,* vol. 2 (Chicago: Moody Press, 1980), p. 664.

CHAPTER 4

Three Prophets and the City

In 1984 Debbie and I lived in Brooklyn. We planned to start City View Baptist Church. We had a meeting place on Flatbush Avenue in the geographic center of Brooklyn. We had ten thousand church brochures to distribute. We did not know anyone, however. We had no people but with church brochures in hand, I hit the streets to find them. It was a beautiful autumn day. I began going door to door and street corner to street corner. The very first day out in my search for souls, I came to the corner of Bedford Avenue and Avenue D. Mrs. Green, Carter, and a man called "Runt" stood talking. I introduced myself and gave each one a brochure. They gladly accepted my invitation, and Carter took my hand and led me away from his friends. He began crying. He squeezed my hand hard, leading me to a black railing over which he leaned. He finally let go of my hand, and he grabbed the railing with equal force, and said, "I need Jesus, I need Jesus." Tears flowed from his eyes. I explained to Carter the gospel of salvation; he said he understood. I led him in a "sinner's prayer." After his prayer, with tears still in his eyes, I asked him, "Carter, where would you go if you died today?" He looked at me and said, "I would go straight to hell." I said to him, "Romans 10:13 says, 'Whosoever shall call upon the name of the Lord shall be saved.' Where do saved people go?" He responded, "Heaven." I then asked, "If you sincerely just called upon the name of the Lord, where would you go?" He looked at me as if he was struggling with doubt. He wanted to believe, but heaven for him seemed too good to be true. I saw his conflict. Carter had lived a life of much drinking up to that point. "We are saved by God's grace through faith, not feeling, Carter," I said. Just then his eyes lit up and he said, "I would go to heaven! Come, let's tell my wife." We walked up a few blocks on Avenue D to where Carter lived, and he introduced me to his wife, Vernice. She was very thin and looked sick. I sat in the living room and heard the trials they were passing through. He had lung cancer caused by cigarette smoking, and one half of one of his lungs had already been removed. Vernice had kidney failure and spent twelve hours a week on a dialysis machine. This was the first of many visits I made with this precious family. I met their two boys, Kevin, seven, and Kenton, five. During the next year, Vernice's condition worsened as she went in and out of the hospital. Carter's cancer recurred also, and he was in and out of several hospitals. Within a year, Vernice died. Two weeks to the day after she died, Carter followed her to heaven. Both funerals were held in our church. It was not an easy task telling their two young boys at their kitchen table that they would never see their parents again. I comforted them with God's Word and prayed that He would show Himself faithful to His promises: "When my father and my mother forsake me, then the Lord will take me up" (Psalm 27:10). Meeting Carter and Vernice at the very start of our ministry in New York City demonstrated to me the great needs that do exist in our cities. People are sick often because of their sin. Children grow up without the presence of their parents for many reasons. The Lord showed me that He wants His Word to go forth upon the streets of the city. We must not run from this task. The Old Testament prophets deal much with urban issues. The problems and sins of the nation took root in the cities and then affected and infected the nation. Here we shall consider three Old Testament prophets that spoke about the city. They give us hope today that we can see souls in the city turn to our Savior.

ISAIAH: GOD'S WORD CRIES FROM THE CITY

"O Zion, that bringest good tidings, get thee up into the high mountain; O Jerusalem, that bringest good tidings, lift up thy voice with strength; lift it up, be not afraid; say unto the cities of Judah, Behold your God!" (Isaiah 40:9). In Isaiah 40, Isaiah prophetically predicted Israel's return from their seventy-year Babylonian captivity. God comforted His people with His promises as they anticipated the long and dangerous journey from their land of slavery. Along the way, God promised that His glory would be revealed (Isaiah 40:3-5). His Word would endure (Isaiah 40:6-8). God Himself would reign (Isaiah 40:9-11) as He personally led Israel out of Babylon and through the wilderness to rebuild the city of Jerusalem. God promised this tiny group of people, like a much-despised "worm" (Isaiah 41:14) in their world, that He would remove every obstacle in their return and reveal His glory. God would blaze a trail for this nation, raising valleys, leveling mountains, and making the road straight and smooth! God would make them into a "new sharp threshing instrument having teeth" so that they could overcome every mountainous problem they faced (Isaiah 41:15). God would "do a new thing" in making a way through the wilderness and providing "rivers in the desert" (Isaiah 43:19). God promised to "open rivers in high places" and to "pour water upon him that [was] thirsty, and floods upon the dry ground" (Isaiah 41:18; 44:3). These promises of water in the wilderness speak of God pouring out "his spirit upon" a nation in desperate need of inner strength. God promised His presence when they passed through the deep waters and hot fires (Isaiah 43:2). No matter the dangers, God's people have His companionship during any calamity.

This promise for the power of the Holy Spirit is for us today. We can take on mighty mountains even though we are insignificant "worms"! God can make us something we are not when His Holy Spirit is poured out upon us. He does not merely *give* us an instrument to thresh the mountain with, He *makes* us an instrument to crumble the mountain to dust, and then He can remove every remnant of the problem. What would you attempt for God if you knew you would not fail? What mountain would you seek to overcome if you knew that God would give you the power to overcome it? Would you plant a church in a city or needy community? Would you seek to assist a church planter, teach a class, work with teens, start a homeless ministry, or sing in a choir? We must thirst for God and ask Him to pour the water of His Holy Spirit on our thirsty souls!

As Israel returned to their land, God challenged his people to return to the city and rebuild it into a *place of strength*. God Himself gave a divine commission for the city. He spoke to the city personally. God desired the city of Jerusalem to be a center of spiritual and moral strength. "Get thee up into the high mountain; O Jerusalem, that bringest good tidings, lift up thy voice with strength." In our day cities are known as places of crime, violence, sin, and shame. Some Christians flee from the city like one avoided a leper in ancient times. Many feel that the cities are beyond hope. This is not God's heart or desire. God is able to rebuild the ruins of the city. He can restore the city from ashes into a place of beauty so that the nation can be led into paths of godliness (Isaiah 61:3). He told the nation of Israel upon returning from captivity to go back into the city and reconstruct it to a place of strength. The city before captivity had become the center of idolatry and was the focus of His wrath, but God in His mercy would make Jerusalem a voice of truth and good news for a nation that would need much encouragement. God could turn their "Ground Zero" into a "garden of the Lord," full of "joy and gladness" (Isaiah 51:3). The broken-down walls of Jerusalem and the burned temple could "break forth into joy" and "sing together . . . for the Lord hath comforted his people, he hath redeemed Jerusalem" (Isaiah 52:9). God promised them, "And they shall build the old wastes, they shall raise up the former desolations, and they shall repair the waste cities, the desolations of many generations" (Isaiah 61:4).

Is it unreasonable for us to believe that God can use us to rebuild broken-down things in our cities today? God can use us to rebuild broken lives, homes, and churches!

God also exhorts the city to be a *proclaimer of salvation.* The city sets the standards for a nation. What the city is, the nation is in process of becoming. God desired for the city of Jerusalem to proclaim the message of the coming Messiah to all the cities of Judah. God commanded the city of Jerusalem to lead the way in speaking forth the Word of God to the other cities of their nation. God has a heart to reach key population centers and to let them be the center and lamp of the evangelization of a nation! In a sense, God was recommissioning Jerusalem after Israel's captivity to be His voice of comfort and boldness to the land. We need to overcome our fears and go to the city proclaiming, "Behold your God!" As the city gets right with God, then the voice of the city spreads the message of salvation to the rest of the nation.

What a message we have, for we can proclaim, "Behold God, our *Sovereign King!*" "Behold, the Lord God will come with strong hand, and his arm shall rule for him: behold, his reward is with him, and his work before him" (Isaiah 40:10). Jesus is coming to rule and reign and He will come with His reward.

We also can boldly announce, "Behold God, our *Shepherd King!*" "He shall feed his flock like a shepherd: he shall gather the lambs with his arm, and carry them in his bosom, and shall gently lead those that are with young" (Isaiah 40:11). God will feed and lead His people with the gentle strength of a shepherd. Tenderness floods this passage as we see our Shepherd care for the defenseless and carry the directionless. God loves the little lambs and leads those with young.

The ultimate fulfillment of these verses will occur during the millennial and eternal kingdom of Christ. The immediate fulfillment of this Isaiah passage took place when Ezra, Zerubbabel, and Nehemiah led the Jewish captives out of captivity to restore the temple and the walls of Jerusalem. "They shall build the old wastes, they shall raise up the former desolations, and they shall repair the waste cities, the desolations of many generations" (Isaiah 61:4).

In our "pit bull culture," where violence is glamorized and abuse is commonplace, people in our cities need to see the gentle strength of Jesus, our Shepherd King, who has given His life for the sheep. Would not our nation be transformed if our cities were places of spiritual strength and proclaimers of the glorious salvation that is in Christ? Yes, we need to be in our cities, challenging people to surrender to Him, the good, great, and chief Shepherd of our souls (John 10:11; Hebrews 13:20; I Peter 5:4).

Between Thirty-first Street and Thirty-third Street on Eighth Avenue in Manhattan stands the main post office for New York City. It is open twenty-four hours a day, seven days a week. This makes it unique. No matter what hour of the day you enter this post office, people stand in line to obtain services and others are moving here and there. Outside this post office is emblazoned the mail carrier's motto: "Neither snow nor rain nor heat nor gloom of night stays these couriers from the swift completion of their appointed rounds." What a statement of commitment! This same zeal ought to characterize children of God and our desire to carry the good news of our Savior to the lost all around us. We are commissioned and commanded by God to announce this news to all the world: "Behold the Lamb of God, which taketh away the sins of the world!"

JEREMIAH: GOD'S SALVATION REACHES THE CITY

Jeremiah is a Christlike prophet. Like Jesus, Jeremiah preached that the temple had become a den of robbers. "Is this house, which is called by my name, become a den of robbers in your eyes?" (Jeremiah 7:11). Like Jesus, he had a tender heart for his people. "Oh that my head were waters, and mine eyes a fountain of tears, that I might weep day and night for the slain of the daughter of my people"

(Jeremiah 9:1). Like Jesus, Jeremiah had a burning passion and an unquenchable zeal to preach. "But his word was in mine heart as a burning fire shut up in my bones, and I was weary with forbearing, and I could not stay" (Jeremiah 20:9). Like Jesus, he had a burden for the cities of Judah and the streets of Jerusalem.

There is an intrigue and mystery to the streets of a major city. The very mention of certain streets conjures up images of poverty and plenty, of sin and satin. When you hear "Broadway," you think of lights and entertainment. When you hear "Wall Street," you think of business suits and the stock exchange. When you hear "Pennsylvania Avenue," you think of the White House, where our president resides. New York City has sixty-four hundred miles of city streets; no doubt Jerusalem in Jeremiah's day had streets similar to the modern streets in our cities.

In Jeremiah 7:17 we see first a *question about the city streets.* "Seest thou not what they do in the cities of Judah and in the streets of Jerusalem?" In Jeremiah 7, we see Jeremiah, standing in the gate of Solomon's temple as he proclaimed God's Word to those who came and worshiped. From within the temple he pointed his finger outside to the streets of the city and asked a sobering question: "Do you see what is going on out there? Do you see the idolatry practiced fearlessly on the streets? (Jeremiah 7:18-20). Do you see the flagrant and frequent disregard of the Word of God?" Sin and rebellion were committed openly and obstinately by all: children, fathers, and mothers. Jeremiah pleaded with his people to see what was taking place and become stirred to a holy wrath against the sin that offended God's holiness.

God then told Jeremiah to go into these idolatrous thoroughfares and make a *proclamation to the city streets*. "Then the Lord said unto me, Proclaim all these words in the cities of Judah, and in the streets of Jerusalem, saying, Hear ye the words of this covenant, and do them" (Jeremiah 11:6). People are not ashamed to sin on the streets. Believers should not be afraid to speak the truth of God on the streets! Drug dealers openly advertise their product on the streets. Before I was a Christian, I attended many rock concerts in Central Park. While waiting for the concerts to begin, drug dealers would publicly sell their merchandise. "T.H.C., black beauties, acid, marijuana," they would declare. Christian, do not be afraid to preach the good news of Jesus Christ on the streets. Preaching Christ in New York City has changed my life. I have received joy unspeakable in distributing gospel tracts on the street and in preaching in the subways and sometimes on the street corners. My heart has been stirred while holding sidewalk services and seeing God's Word go forth on the streets where sin is evident and rampant.

I will never forget one occasion, witnessing on the streets of Borough Park, Brooklyn. The neighborhood is an orthodox Jewish community. While we distributed tracts, some of the people would take them, rip them up, spit on them, step on them, or do all the above! After a few minutes, many of the Jewish residents and store workers gathered around us and asked us to leave. They tried to grab all of our tracts in order to destroy them. As we began to go, they said, "Do not come back. Tell us right now that you will not come back, or we will beat you up right now." They even began to pick up rocks to throw at us. During this confusion, one young man did stop, and looking me in the face, he asked, "Is your Jesus coming back again?" I answered, "Yes." He then made one of the saddest statements I have ever heard anyone make. "If He comes back again, we will kill Him again." Then he tried to spit in my face. In the streets of the city we can reach all the people of the city.

God also told Jeremiah of *destruction upon the city streets.* "Wherefore my fury and mine anger was poured forth, and was kindled in the cities of Judah and in the streets of Jerusalem; and they are wasted and desolate, as at this day" (Jeremiah 44:6). "The city was broken up" (Jeremiah 52:7; 39:2; II Kings 25:3-4). After two years of Babylonian attacks, Jerusalem was destroyed. The Book of Lamentations gives a descriptive view of the desolation evident upon the city streets. "Mine eyes do fail with tears, my bowels are troubled, my liver is poured upon the earth, for the destruction of the daughter of my people; because the children and the sucklings swoon in the streets of the city. They say to their mothers, Where is corn and wine? when they swooned as the wounded in the streets of the city, when their soul was poured out into their mothers' bosom" (Lamentations 2:11-12). Jeremiah reveals to us homeless mothers and children, fainting, hungering, and nearly dying on the streets of the city. It is no different today. Ten thousand children are born addicted to drugs and alcohol every year in New York City. Homelessness, despair, and sorrow are a way of life to a whole culture of people on our modern city streets.

God promised to Jeremiah *salvation on the city streets.* "Thus saith the Lord; Again there shall be heard in this place, which ye say shall be desolate without man and without beast, even in the cities of Judah, and in the streets of Jerusalem, that are desolate, without man, and without inhabitant, and without beast, the voice of joy, and the voice of gladness, the voice of the bridegroom, and the voice of the bride, the voice of them that shall say, Praise the Lord of hosts: for the Lord is good; for his mercy endureth for ever" (Jeremiah 33:10-11a). The ultimate fulfillment of this passage will be in the millennial reign of Jesus Christ, when He rules in Jerusalem executing "judgment and righteousness" (Jeremiah 33:15). The immediate fulfillment happened during the days of Nehemiah: God brought a revival "into the street that was before the water gate" when the people asked Ezra to "bring the book of the law of Moses, which the Lord had commanded to Israel" (Nehemiah 8:1). What a scene as children, fathers, and mothers stood in the streets of Jerusalem to hear the Word of God read, explained, and applied to their lives! That sight thrills my soul—urban residents hungered in ancient times to hear the Word of God on the streets of the city. Living water flooded the hearts of those who stood at the Water Gate. God is able to bring salvation today where destruction resides. By the grace of God we can hear our city streets reverberate with praise and echo with the sounds of joy as we go with the gospel.

A young man in our church named Chris went with me onto the streets to witness. We ministered God's Word in the heart of Brooklyn in a drug-infested area. Music blared, horns honked, and people scurried back and forth from the apartment buildings that filled the community. When we gave a gospel tract to a young lady named Gina, she expressively lamented our efforts as she told us, "Why did I have to meet you? I am on my way to buy marijuana and I know I shouldn't!" We interrupted her plans to ruin her life. We began giving Gina the gospel and challenged her to repent from her sins and not to buy the marijuana. Christ was the one she should seek. We quoted Psalm 1 to her: "Blessed is the man that walketh not in the counsel of the ungodly, nor standeth in the way of sinners, nor sitteth in the seat of the scornful. But his delight is in the law of the Lord; and in his law doth he meditate day and night." She listened to us and she turned around from where she had planned to go. We walked a couple of blocks with Gina, but eventually we separated from her, and I asked Chris, "Do you think she will go buy that pot?" He said, "I am afraid to say, but she probably will." A few weeks later, after our Sunday evening service, the phone rang. It was Gina. She cried loudly into the phone. She kept repeating, "Do you remember me? Are you for real? Do *you* remember me? Are you a *real* Christian?" I calmed her down and spoke to her about her soul. Gina put her faith in the Lord Jesus Christ to save her from sin. It was a joy to baptize her as well and she grew in the Lord.

JONAH: GOD'S MAN RUNS FROM THE CITY

The Book of Jonah contains three great characters: God, Jonah, and Nineveh. "Now the word of the Lord came unto Jonah the son of Amittai, saying, Arise, go to Nineveh, that great city, and cry against it; for their wickedness is come up before me" (Jonah 1:1-2). Nineveh was the capital of the Assyrian empire. Outwardly, Nineveh was a beautiful city. Militarily, Nineveh was an invincible city. Spiritually, however, Nineveh was lost in sin and within days of God's judgment. Our gracious God takes the initiative in urban ministry even to Gentile cities renowned for violence and ripe for judgment. The wickedness of Nineveh was evident to Him, and He called a prophet to carry His message of deliverance. The difficulty and wickedness of a place is not an excuse to run but a reason to go. Jonah clearly heard God's call to go to this city, but he ran from God's clear call.

In Jonah 1 we see that *you can run from God but you cannot hide*. Jonah disobeyed God as he harbored serious cultural hang-ups against the pagan Gentiles known throughout the world for their violence. Jonah thought God should destroy Nineveh rather than save it. Although Jonah's name means "dove," and God called him to be an ambassador of peace, he brought trouble and not peace to those around him because he ran from God. A whole ship was in trouble in a storm because of his stubborn spirit. This story reminds us that people who run from God do amazingly reckless deeds. The ship's crew found the prophet sleeping down in the sides of the ship, but because he refused to pray and surrender his will to God, Jonah counseled them to "cast me forth into the sea" (Jonah 1:12). Does sin not cause God's people to speak absurdly? Getting thrown overboard into a stormy sea seemed better to Jonah than simply praying and obeying God's clear call. Not only did God hunt the prophet down by the storm and the shipmen but finally God prepared a great fish to swallow him. As this headstrong runner slunk down a slippery super slide of a different sort, he still clung to his racial bias against the people of Nineveh. Jonah refused to pray as he slid into the belly of the great fish. Jonah's backslidden state had reached such deep proportions that it took him three days before he could bring himself to pray from the belly of the fish!

Jonah 2 shows that *a disobedient preacher can stop running from God*. Jonah presumptuously and knowingly "went down to Joppa" (Jonah

1:3). Next, he went "down into the sides of the ship" (Jonah 1:5). Humanly speaking, Jonah completely controlled his life. Even someone called to preach can run from God and foolishly think he controls his pathway, but the further he goes away from God in willful disobedience the more he loses control. The law of sowing and reaping always kicks in. Although Jonah experienced what it was to be cast down and to feel cast out of God's sight, God in mercy maintained breath in him, and he finally *looked up,* remembered God, and prayed in faith. God's grace, available for the whole city of Nineveh, also existed for Jonah. Jonah's prayer pierced like a javelin through the whale's belly all the way into heaven and God heard him! Perhaps he realized there was no human way out of that fish; prayer was the only way out. I have often heard others call this the "school of hard knocks at whale bottom seminary." Jonah's seminary could have been his cemetery if he had not prayed. He surrendered to God and *let go* as the seaweed wrapped around his head and the waves washed over his soul. It often takes deep calamity to realize that we need to get rid of "lying vanities" (Jonah 2:8). Holding on to hateful attitudes kept him back from experiencing the mercy of God. The subtle yet worthless idol to which he clung was a lack of love for all those created in God's image. This same attitude exists today among some believers toward the ethnic multitudes that live in our nation's cities. Do you feverishly hold on to a "deceitful air bubble" that keeps you on the run from God? We must let go of hateful attitudes; we must confess and forsake sinful anxieties, selfish ambitions, and worldly activities. "Lying vanities" come in many packages. Finally, the proud prophet *laid down* his life as one alive from the dead. Jonah remembered the Lord and recognized that God is sovereign in salvation. "I will sacrifice unto thee with the voice of thanksgiving; I will pay that that I have vowed. Salvation is of the Lord" (Jonah 2:9).

Jonah 3 gives us hope that *God in mercy often gives a second chance.* "The word of the Lord came unto Jonah the second time" (Jonah 3:1). In this chapter, everyone is "crying" but in a good way! The words "preach," "preaching" (v. 2), "cried" (v. 4), "proclaimed" (v. 5), and "cry (mightily)" (v. 8) are all the same root Hebrew word. God's voice cried in patient love to Jonah the second time to preach His Word (see also Micah 6:9). Jonah cried in obedience to the people of Nineveh to repent from sin. The Ninevites cried to one another to fast and repent. They then cried "mightily unto God" to turn from their "evil way, and from the violence that [was] in their hands" (Jonah 3:8). We ought to maintain a confidence that when God speaks His truth to us, He will speak His truth through us to effect the desire that He has ordained. Citywide revivals will not happen through human instrumentality alone but by God's divine decree. God's Word will not return void, for He says that His Word "shall accomplish that which I please, and it shall prosper in the thing whereto I sent it" (Isaiah 55:11).

It seems that all of God's creation obeyed God in Jonah except the prophet himself. The shipmen cried in faith to God (1:14), the city of Nineveh cried to God (3:5), the fish, the gourd, and the east wind all obeyed God (4:6-8). This book ends with Jonah selfishly sitting outside the city, angry at God. The abrupt ending does not give me confidence that Jonah repented again of his unloving ways. Jonah loved temporal plants more than he loved the eternal souls of Ninevites. His heart remained silent to God's final appeal for compassion. In comparison to Jonah's, God's heartbeat for lost souls in large urban centers rings loudly: "And should not I spare Nineveh, that great city?" (4:11). This brief book rebukes us concerning our selfish attitudes that cause us to refuse to recognize the importance of reaching cities that influence the world. The Book of Jonah continues to speak of God's desire to send His messengers to wicked places.

In Washington Square Park in the middle of Greenwich Village, Manhattan, an archway stands in memory of our first president, George Washington. His words are engraved on the top of that arch:

> *Let us raise a standard to which the wise and the honest can repair: the event is in the hand of God.*

Washington probably meant that the founding of our nation was by the power of "the hand of God." No doubt this Founding Father desired our nation to be an example of freedom where other lovers of freedom could come and "repair" from their despair. I have taken this quote and applied it to our church in the midst of this Greenwich Village area that is a bastion of atheism, Marxism, and humanistic thought that forgets God. Our church and the founding of our church is in the hand of God. We desire our church to be a place where the wise and honest can find spiritual rest in Jesus Christ in order to repair their souls. Like Isaiah, we should want God's Word to cry from the city. Like Jeremiah, we should work so that God's salvation reaches the city streets. Unlike Jonah, we should refuse to run. Will you come to join us in reaching the city? It is an event in the hand of God!

CHAPTER 5

The Lord's Voice Cries to the City

September 11, 2001, now stands for unspeakable terror and chilling devastation. This date stands as the most infamous day in American history; it is being called "America Under Attack." An unprecedented act of war was perpetrated against the United States; it was a second Pearl Harbor. The relaxed, self-confident attitude of America disappeared under rubble in a few moments of time; the aura of American invincibility crumbled to the ground in a plume of smoke in two of her greatest cities, New York and Washington, D.C. Two hijacked airplanes leaving Boston intentionally crashed into the famous 110-floor World Trade Center Towers in the heart of New York City's downtown Manhattan, the world's financial nerve center. In a scene reminiscent of a movie, balls of fire filled the sky in this real-life event. The first plane, a Boeing 767, struck the north tower at 8:48 A.M. somewhere between the ninety-sixth and 103rd floors. The second plane, also a Boeing 767, struck the south tower somewhere between the eighty-seventh and ninety-third floors at 9:03 A.M. Another hijacked plane collided, like an ax into a birthday cake, into the Pentagon in Washington, D.C., America's military nerve center. A fourth hijacked plane crashed in a Pennsylvania field outside of Pittsburgh. All four planes were hijacked without a bullet being fired. The four planes contained a total of two hundred sixty-six souls, who all perished. Evidently, nineteen hijackers overcame the crews with knives. President George Bush said, "The resolve of our great nation is being tested. These acts shattered steel, but they cannot dent the steel of American resolve." New York mayor Rudy Giuliani said of this day, "I have a sense a horrendous number of lives are lost." These murderous deeds undoubtedly were the work of extremist Muslim terrorists who hate America and Israel; they are dedicated to destroying our freedoms as well as our resolve to help the nation of Israel. I am writing as the events unfold.

The two commercial jetliners that sliced right through these mighty skyscrapers caused fire to rage uncontrolled in the heart of those buildings. The planes were filled with fuel sufficient for flight across America and therefore behaved like bombs. When the first plane hit 1 World Trade Center, the north tower, panic gripped those trapped above the blaze and many who were frantic tragically jumped from the building to their deaths. Cell phone calls were made from the top of the towers to loved ones expressing love for the last time. A surprising number actually made it out of the building to safety. Many workers in 2 World Trade Center, the south tower, who felt the shock of the first plane crashing, began to leave. Some, however, stayed because they were told that their building was stable. "You can go back to your floor; the building is secure," they were assured. Some had begun to leave but sadly returned to their floor. This false message resulted in death, for Tower 2 would fall first. They had less than an hour to make a life and death decision. Leslie, a member of our church, works for Morgan Stanley, which was in Tower 2. Thankfully, she left when she knew of problems in Tower 1. In her descent, she made it to the thirteenth floor by the time the plane hit her building at 9:03.

As the buildings blazed, triage centers were set up in front of the Hilton Millennium Hotel across the street from the World Trade Center. This seemed to be a haven of safety, but it would soon be a place of death as well. Workers sat on the sidewalk with serious burns and blood streaming from open wounds. As injured people streamed out of the burning infernos, rescue workers raced into them not suspecting what was coming next. Within an hour, both structures fell to the ground like a house of cards. Windows rattled and burst, floors trembled and cracked, debris rained from the sky, and the buildings folded, killing many. The south tower fell first at 9:59 A.M. The north tower crumbled at 10:28 A.M. Pandemonium ensued. It seemed incomprehensible that this could happen. The death toll was immediately presumed to be in the thousands; within seventy-two hours there were 4,763 people estimated missing, including more than 300 firefighters, 40 police officers, and as many as 200 Port Authority employees. By December 28, 2001, 3,163 people had died, or were missing and presumed dead, not including the nineteen hijackers. These two towers of power and strength were suddenly eliminated without warning. Tons of debris filled the street. Black smoke billowed from the heart of New York's financial district. Taxis slammed into buildings. Many ran away from the tidal wave of terror only to be engulfed in the debris and smoke. A beautiful sun-splashed day became completely black. Many who made it out alive thought their life was over. Other buildings around the two largest buildings in Manhattan also caught fire and raged out of control. Incredulous people ran out of downtown Manhattan in hysteria, panic, and tears. A firefighter expressed his hopelessness by saying, "There's nothing anybody can do."[1] Bridges and tunnels were shut down. The nation stopped to watch. We all knew that we could have been there. All New Yorkers, but also many other Americans, felt a close connection with the World Trade Center. So many of us had visited the observation deck, and so many of us knew one of the 50,000 people who worked there. An incredible mountain of metal now filled downtown Manhattan in this nightmare beyond human comprehension for any American.

The police, firemen, EMS workers, civilians, doctors, and nurses throughout the city demonstrated great heroism during the day of attack. Great tragedy always results in human strength and the opportunity to overcome the trial of the moment. A man named Louis carried his coworker fifty-four flights down the stairwell in ninety-degree heat. He stayed with her until she was out of the building and at a place of safety. He was one of thousands who bravely sought to save someone else. The human will can withstand and overcome incredible odds. Times of such difficulty also have a way of bringing people together. The city of New York faced this calamity with unity and dignity. Help also poured into our city from across the nation.

In times like this, what should be our response? We ought to have compassion upon the victims and their families. My heart breaks for those who died in this act of terrorist cowardice. Seeing people jump out of the doomed towers was unspeakably tragic. The pictures of lost or missing loved ones hanging around the city showed so many young lives taken. Many died as unsuspecting victims; others died as heroes trying to save lives. My heart aches for those who lost loved ones in the carnage. What can we say to people at moments like this? Jesus commented about such a trial in His own day when Pilate ruthlessly killed Galileans. He said that those Galileans who died were not greater sinners than those who did not die. Others in the city of Siloam were killed when the tower in Siloam fell. Those who died were not greater sinners "above all men that dwelt in Jerusalem" (Luke 13:4). In times like this, we need to challenge the living to prepare for the day of their death. Jesus reminds us that when such trials do occur, we all need to get right with our God and repent: "I tell you, . . . but, except ye repent, ye shall all likewise perish" (Luke 13:5). We must take a long look and realize that eternal salvation is a more pressing need than even physical life. We must resist the temptation to get angry at God; rather, we must see the big picture and realize that one day our flesh will collapse just like the World Trade Center. Have you forgotten that you, too, must die? "And as it is appointed unto men once to die, but after this the judgment" (Hebrews 9:27). We must be prepared to meet God. God allows judgments to wake us up so that we can be saved. His voice cries so that we can see He is God. The prophet Amos describes those who survived judgment allowed by God but refused to hear His voice: "I have overthrown some of you, as God overthrew Sodom and Gomorrah, and ye were as a firebrand plucked out of the burning: yet have ye not returned unto me, saith the Lord" (Amos 4:11). When trials fall upon a city, we must not become bitter toward God but return to the Lord.

We should realize that this terrorist act was permitted by our almighty, holy, and sovereign God. Although we do not know the mind of God in this, we do know that sin brings His judgment. God's judgments are mysterious, but even the death of Jesus upon the cross shows that God allows and even ordains wicked people to bring about His righteous judgment (Acts 4:26-28). In the Old Testament, the Lord used unbelieving Arab nations as a rod in His hand to bring judgment upon His people (Habakkuk 1; Micah 6:9). The wrath of man can still praise God, however, and even the darkness and evil that God allows can lead to the skies pouring down righteousness and the earth bringing forth salvation (Isaiah 45:7-8). Although at times of such judgment we should unite, we must also repent. At times of calamity we should be strong to rebuild, but we must also search our heart and turn from sin. Patriotism and national unity are a natural and wholesome response when such an attack strikes at our freedom, but turning to God in genuine repentance and faith, though not so natural, is more necessary. We have killed millions of babies through abortion. We have allowed immorality to increase and abound. We have committed untold atrocities. The Bible clearly states, "Whoremongers and adulterers God will judge" (Hebrews 13:4*b*). We should not be surprised when His judgment comes upon one of America's great cities. God's judgment upon nations in Scripture fell most severely upon the cities, whether Babylon, Nineveh, Jerusalem, or Samaria. Our only hope is to turn to God. "Turn us, O God of our salvation, and cause thine anger toward us to cease. . . . Wilt thou not revive us again: that thy people may rejoice in thee? Shew us thy mercy, O Lord, and grant us thy salvation" (Psalm 85:4-7). In America, like Babylon of old, we have taken safety and security for granted; we are "given to pleasures" and have said in our hearts, "I am, and [there is] *none else beside me*" (Isaiah 47:8). I do not know if America is as ready for judgment as Babylon, but when God is ready to send judgment, no one can stop it (Isaiah 47:11).

A people who realize judgment is impending will be more ready to repent and pray for revival. God told Habakkuk that judgment upon the nation of Judah was imminent. Babylon was going to come like a desert wind upon Judah and would gather prisoners and carry them away into captivity just like wind gathers up sand in its fist: "they shall gather the captivity as the sand" (Habakkuk 1:9*b*). At first, Habakkuk wondered at God's justice. How could God use the wicked to devour men more righteous than they (Habakkuk 1:13)? God then assured His prophet that although Babylon would judge Judah, God would also judge Babylon (Habakkuk 2). Habakkuk then responded to Babylon's coming destruction upon his nation by praying for revival. "O Lord, I have heard thy speech, and was afraid: O Lord, revive thy work in the midst of the years, in the midst of the years make known; in wrath remember mercy" (Habakkuk 3:2). A people who understand the reality of God's judgment will pray for God to reveal His presence, revive His work, and remember His mercy.

The Book of Micah presents a special burden for the city. Micah was a country boy with an urban burden. He was a Morasthite. Moresheth was a small Judean town about twenty-five miles southwest of Jerusalem. One may grow up in a small town and get a large burden to be a voice for God in the city. Although Micah was not originally from Jerusalem or Samaria, he saw the influence large cities had upon these two nations, and he was deeply distressed by what he saw.

Micah realized that the capital cities were the heartbeat of the land that affected the nation. "He prophesied 'concerning Samaria and Jerusalem,' the capitals of the two kingdoms, that is to say, concerning all Israel, the fate of which was determined by the circumstances and fates of the two capitals."[2] He writes in order to turn these cities back to God. He warns them of coming judgment but he also promises them the coming of the ultimate deliverer (Micah 5:2). Micah's prophecy challenges us not to neglect the cities of our nation and world, for what cities are, nations become. Key cities still determine the ultimate destiny of a nation.

Cities were the centers of sin and the fountainheads of the nation's moral and religious apostasy. "What is the transgression of Jacob? is it not Samaria? and what are the high places of Judah? are they not Jerusalem?" (Micah 1:5). The capital cities "apparently 'set the pace' for the rest of Israel and Judah, with the worst sins being committed in the largest urban areas."[3] "The capitals of the two kingdoms are the authors of the apostasy, as the centers and sources of the corruption which has spread from them over the kingdoms."[4] The "high places" represented religious idolatry. The religious sins that affected the nation of Judah were most deeply rooted in the city of Jerusalem. The false prophets of Jerusalem influenced the entire nation. Jeremiah wrote, "For from the prophets of Jerusalem is profaneness gone forth into all the land" (Jeremiah 23:15). The "transgression of Jacob" points to the moral rebellion of the people. This rebellion centered in the city and spewed out to the rest of the Northern Kingdom of Israel.

These cities that were the fountainheads of sin would become the focus of judgment. God promised that He would "make Samaria as an heap of the field" and that He would bring a judgment that would reveal the very foundations of the city (Micah 1:6). Micah saw the two great cities of Israel and Judah bring decay to the nation and realized that these two influential cities determined the destiny of all Israel. With this burden, "the word of the Lord" (Micah 1:1) came to him.

Micah revealed God's heart for the city in Micah 6:9. "The Lord's voice crieth unto the city, and the man of wisdom shall see thy name: hear ye the rod, and who hath appointed it." The *Lord's* voice cries to the city. God wants the city to hear His majestic voice! "The voice of the Lord is powerful; the voice of the Lord is full of majesty. The voice of the Lord breaketh the cedars. . . . The voice of the Lord divideth the flames of fire" (Psalm 29:4-5, 7). The word "crieth" is a powerful word that emphasizes urgency. It is often used of man crying out to God: "This poor man cried, and the Lord . . . saved him out of all his troubles" (Psalm 34:6). God's entreaty is a compelling cry over a critical and chronic need. In Micah 6:9 we see God crying out to man! Oh, the mighty love of God! If God is going to cry today, it will be through His servants preaching His Word. God's Word cried out to Jonah. Jonah cried out to the inhabitants of Nineveh. The people of Nineveh cried out to God. When God's word cries in truth through His servants, then men will cry earnestly to God and repent. Let's see three reasons that God's voice cries to the city.

PACESETTERS OF WICKEDNESS

God's voice cries to the city because the city sets the pace for *wickedness* in the nation. The sins of the city do not cause God to retreat but to reach out. God seeks to attack the problem of sin at its source. God had commanded Jonah to go to Nineveh because of their wickedness. "Arise, go to Nineveh, that great city, and cry against it; for their wickedness is come up before me" (Jonah 1:2).

God's voice cried to the cities of Samaria and Jerusalem in Micah's day because of the idolatry, covetousness, oppression, violence, and corruption of the land. Because cities set the pace for sin in a nation's culture, it is imperative that we bring the solution for sin, the gospel of Jesus Christ, to the source of sin. The common people were defrauded by the selfish and powerful: "They covet fields, and take them by violence; and houses, and take them away: so they oppress a man and his house, even a man and his heritage" (Micah 2:2). False prophets and greedy priests denied the true power of God by preaching a false peace for financial profit: "Thus saith the Lord concerning the prophets that make my people err, that bite with their teeth, and cry, Peace" (Micah 3:5). Micah 3:11 says that the "priests thereof teach for hire, and the prophets thereof divine for money: yet will they lean upon the Lord, and say, Is not the Lord among us? none evil can come upon us." They piously boasted of trusting in God, maintaining a form of godliness. Their message gave a false security to the people and failed to direct them to the Lord, who alone gives true security—eternal life. In fact, these false prophets were motivated by covetous desires. Their business practices were full of fraud. People bought and sold with dishonest words and deceitful weights. "Shall I count them pure with the wicked balances, and with the bag of deceitful weights? For the rich men thereof are full of violence, and the inhabitants thereof have spoken lies, and their tongue is deceitful in their mouth" (Micah 6:11-12). The political rulers also behaved corruptly and gave themselves over to bribery. "The prince asketh . . . for a reward; and the great man, he uttereth his mischievous desire: so they wrap it up" (Micah 7:3). The family was broken down and disintegrated through disrespect. "For the son dishonoureth the father, the daughter riseth up against her mother, the daughter in law against her mother in law; a man's enemies are the men of his own house" (Micah 7:6). As I read these verses, it seems that Micah lived in some modern day city, for the problems that plague man and our current cities have not changed. In the midst of this wickedness, God had not given up. He still had His man crying out to these wicked cities, pleading for them to repent!

We live in a violent and immoral society. Murder, assaults, physical abuse, child rape, gang activity, sexual assaults, robbery, domestic violence, suicide, and many other violent crimes pervade our culture. Since the attack upon America, we now fear terrorist violence. There are forty thousand suicides annually in the United States. Every fourteen hours a young person between the ages of eleven and nineteen takes his or her life. More than six million Americans are in our criminal justice system every day. Every thirty-six hours a police officer is killed in the line of duty; every twenty-two hours a police officer commits suicide from despair. The cost for us to have a justice system is nearly a hundred million dollars annually, and things are not improving. More prisons and jails are built each year, and as soon as they are built they are filled to capacity. Children ages 8 to 17 commit more violent felonies than any other age group. It is a violent generation whose "teeth are as swords, and their jaw teeth as knives" (Proverbs 30:14). This is the fourth generation described by the Scripture in Proverbs 30:11-14. There is no fifth generation because that society that reaches this fourth stage will be destroyed from within.[5]

In the summer of 1984, Debbie and I had just moved into New York City. One day, a lady from the neighborhood reported grim news. A man had stabbed and killed his wife in the presence of his two teen daughters, and then he had jumped from the roof of their building. Someone was needed to preach the funeral. It was my second funeral. The afternoon of the funeral service the church was full and the emotion was high. One lady sang a song: "There Is Peace in the Valley." She repeated that line many times until nearly the whole congregation wailed and loudly cried. They cried because of a lack of peace. God's peace seemed like a distant reality to that congregation. After I preached, the family came forward to view the deceased for the last time. The oldest daughter just stood over the casket and cried, saying, "I want my mommy." She had to be carried away from the casket, kicking the shoes off her feet as she went. I stood at the head of the casket, a very young pastor with very little experience, and I was overwhelmed with sorrow for those who faced such tragedy that would affect their entire life. It was a moment that remains with me as I saw firsthand the devastation of sin and the destruction of the family.

PEOPLE THAT ARE WISE

God's voice also cries to the city because of the *wise* in the city. "The man of wisdom shall see thy name" (Micah 6:9). Many in the city are deaf to God's voice. The hum of business and the whispers of Satan drown the mighty voice of God for the foolish. The wise person, however, sees God's name. This speaks of salvation. Seeing His name speaks of believing; the one who believes in Him sees the glory that is in His name! When a soul responds to God's grace and listens to His voice, he will see the power of His name. The Lord's voice cries to reveal His name. Who can comprehend the glory and unsearchable nature of God's name? His name reveals His eternal and infinite character. There are many voices that compete with God's voice; many things compete with a man seeing His name, the name that is above every name. The wise man tunes out all the stations to listen to God's voice; he tunes out all other channels to get a clear vision of God's name. Yes, the wise man tunes out the sights and sounds of the city that drown out the beauty of God's person. There are some that will hear and be saved in our cities! The wise realizes the only alternative in a decaying culture is to put God's name in his eye. "Therefore I will look unto the Lord; I will wait for the God of my salvation: my God will hear me. Rejoice not against me, O mine enemy: when I fall, I shall arise; when I sit in darkness, the Lord shall be a light unto me" (Micah 7:7-8).

On considering a place of ministry one never humanly desires to expose himself to the sin, crime, and violence of a place like New York City. A place that resembles a malignant growth? A place that resembles a volcano spewing its violence all around? Why live in a place that is a target for terrorist attack? Why live in a place of constant little irritations? Why live in a place where I cannot park my car on the street without moving it often in order not to get a parking ticket? Why live in a city where getting parking tickets is a way of life? Why live in a city where I cannot leave a child's car seat in a vehicle overnight because some thief will steal it to buy $10 worth of crack? The answer is "the man of wisdom shall see thy name." The people of New York City are a great reason to go! The people are tremendous, and when they trust Christ, they become new creatures in Christ. Ministry is joyous in an urban area.

To me the most difficult aspect of urban ministry has not been starting a church or working to see the church grow. The most torturous part of our ministry has been leaving the people we have grown to love. God had led us to establish City View Baptist Church (1984) in Flatbush, Brooklyn, but our burden was to begin another church in another needy area of New York City. When I resigned from City View Baptist Church in 1989, I preached from I Kings 17:8-9, where the Lord told Elijah to "arise, get thee to Zarephath . . . and dwell there: behold, I have commanded a widow woman there to sustain thee." I am usually not an emotional person and rarely cry publicly. However, during that service, the tears flowed naturally and from many in the congregation. I begged the church to believe God and to have faith in Him that the Lord was directing us to start another church. I also beseeched them to believe that God could provide a pastor for them and that they could provide financially for a pastor. Within a few months, the Lord did direct a good man to pastor the church. We helped the church to call in a new shepherd, and I helped him move into the area and adjust to the church and community. I vividly remember driving away from Flatbush Avenue for the last time as the pastor of this congregation. As I drove out of Flatbush, my heart ached and my eyes filled with tears. Memories of the precious people flooded my heart. My prayer was "Lord lead me and help me to establish another church in this city!" The farthest thing from my mind was to leave this mighty city where so many people would put God's name in their eye. As the people of City View Baptist came to mind, the tears flowed again down my cheeks, for we had worked with many people who had the wisdom to see that God's name is a strong tower that reveals His salvation and sovereignty. Starting and leaving a church is a great lesson in trust because the realization that the church is the Lord's becomes crystal clear, and not just in a theoretical way. The Lord has taken great care of City View Baptist Church since we departed in 1989. Their present pastor, Bryan Taitt, was a former member and deacon of the church, and he has naturally grown into the leadership of that congregation. The people of New York City lead me to say, "I love New York!" God has many who will put His name in their eye.

"Know ye not that the unrighteous shall not inherit the kingdom of God? Be not deceived: neither fornicators, nor idolaters, nor adulterers, nor effeminate, nor abusers of themselves with mankind, nor thieves, nor covetous, nor drunkards, nor revilers, nor extortioners, shall inherit the kingdom of God. And such were some of you: but ye are washed, but ye are sanctified, but ye are justified in the name of the Lord Jesus, and by the Spirit of our God" (I Corinthians 6: 9-11). In our present church in Manhattan, we are a bunch of "such weres"! We have dear folks who love the Lord that were drunkards, drug addicts, prostitutes, motorcycle thieves, cult members, homeless people, and lost religious people. They have put God's name in their eye and have been rescued by the transforming and liberating power of Jesus Christ. Yes, many in the city are wise; this makes ministry in the city a joy.

PLACES APPOINTED FOR GOD'S WRATH

God's voice cries to the city because His *wrath* is against the city. "Hear ye the rod, and who hath appointed it" (Micah 6:9). The rod speaks of the judgment of God. Jerusalem would receive the rod of judgment from Assyria and ultimately Babylon. God would use these heathen nations as a rod in His hand. A man will either see His name or hear the rod of His wrath. Individuals either hear His voice of compassion and come to Him or hear His voice of wrath and fall under His condemnation. Israel had rejected the Lord's *challenge:* "The Lord hath a controversy with his people, and he will plead with Israel" (Micah 6:2). They had forsaken the Lord's *compassion.*

He had redeemed them (Micah 6:4) and had protected them (Micah 6:5). They had also abandoned His clear *counsel* of what He required. "He hath shewed thee, O man, what is good; and what doth the Lord require of thee, but to do justly, and to love mercy, and to walk humbly with thy God?" (Micah 6:8). Because they rejected His challenge, His compassion, His counsel, and even His cry, they would hear His rod of wrath. God uses even heathen nations as a rod of His wrath against other nations and against His disobedient chosen people. Those who reject His voice cannot experience His peace.

Throughout Scripture, cities fell under the rod of God's wrath. Jeremiah wrote about how the Gentile city of Damascus would fall under God's judgment. The Jewish prophet lamented the beautiful city of Damascus: "How is the city of praise not left, the city of my joy! Therefore her young men shall fall in her streets, and all the men of war shall be cut off in that day, saith the Lord of hosts" (Jeremiah 49:25-26). These verses fascinate me because Jeremiah mourns for a pagan city far away from him. This weeping prophet was touched with compassion for the people of a different race than he. We also should have a compassion and concern for cities around our world that experience famine, war, terrorism, and bloodshed. In the aftermath of the events of September 11, 2001, these verses came to life. People from around the country and world mourned for the destruction that hit New York City and aid poured in from all over.

The Book of Nahum deals with God's certain judgment upon the city of Nineveh. This judgment took place about one hundred fifty years after they repented through Jonah's preaching. Nahum 3:19 shows the serious worldwide effect cities possess. Nahum boldly predicted Nineveh's demise without giving them an escape: "There is no healing of thy bruise; thy wound is grievous: all that hear the bruit of thee shall clap the hands over thee: for upon whom hath not thy wickedness passed continually?" None would mourn the utter desolation of this violent city. God's justice would make sure that Nineveh's wickedness would stop corrupting, influencing, and ransacking the rest of the world. This destruction in 612 B.C. was so severe that the ruins of the city were not uncovered until 1842!

The ministry of Jesus Christ is serious. It is a matter of life and death; it is a matter of heaven and hell. The wrath of God, a serious matter, can often be heard. In ancient days one would hear the chariots raging in the streets; the palaces, homes, and temple crackling with flames; and the city walls crumbling to dust. In like fashion, one can hear His wrath upon the city today: the crash of a car, the crack of a bullet, the crackle of the flame, and the crumbling of a building on fire. One can hear the weeping mother and the mourning child. God uses His rod to gain the attention of His creation and bring us to repentance.

On that fateful day of September 11 in America, the *New York Times* reported, "It kept getting worse. The horror arrived in episodic bursts of chilling disbelief, signified first by trembling floors, sharp eruptions, cracked windows. There was the actual unfathomable realization of a gaping, flaming hole in first one of the tall towers, and then the same thing all over again in its twin. There was the merciless sight of bodies helplessly tumbling out, some of them in flames. Finally, the mighty towers themselves were reduced to nothing. Dense plumes of smoke raced through the downtown avenues, coursing between the buildings, shaped like tornadoes on their sides. Every sound was cause for alarm."[6] Yes, *"every sound was cause for alarm."* May America respond to the sound of the rod of God and see His name by repenting of sin and believing in the Lord Jesus Christ.

In the aftermath of September 11 New York City seemed to have less. "It was a city of less. Less traffic, less noise, fewer people, less activity, less momentum, less certainty, less joy. Nothing felt the same, and the most glaring difference was less skyline."[7] In the midst of less, I am praying for more. I pray that God will save more souls and that He will pour down His righteousness and bring forth salvation in the midst of the darkness and evil (Isaiah 45:7-8). I pray that there will be more faith, more dedication, more love, more prayer, and more hope in our city as we move forward. I pray that God will raise up more laborers to enter into this harvest field of souls. I pray for real revival and for God to do more through His faithful people in our city that humanly has less.

Outside of the United Nations near Forty-second Street and First Avenue in New York City, one can find a wall with Isaiah 2:4 inscribed upon it: "They shall beat their swords into plowshares, and their spears into pruninghooks: nation shall not lift up sword against nation, neither shall they learn war any more." Human efforts carried out by the United Nations, no matter how sincere, will never bring fulfillment to this verse. Everyone wants peace, but we cannot "visualize" our way to world peace. Lighting candles will not bring about peace. Neither will nuclear disarmament nor the negotiation of nations bring such peace. Peacekeeping forces or any defense initiative will not secure world peace. The only way man can attain a life of peace is to know Him who is the Prince of peace. We have "peace through the blood of his cross" (Colossians 1:20), and peace is a fruit of the Holy Spirit (Galatians 5:22). World peace will happen only when "the government shall be upon his shoulder," that of our Lord Jesus Christ, who is the "Wonderful, Counsellor, The mighty God, The everlasting Father, The Prince of Peace." Until then, war will continue, and God will use one nation as a rod of His wrath upon another nation. We know that the Battle of Armageddon is still before us; until that battle, war will continue in this land of the dying. Without faith in the Savior, wrath awaits. We must stand in our world and let God use us as His voice in the cities of our world. Some will still put God's name in their eye and be saved. Others will face His rod of wrath. Let's be a voice for our God in our cities, for personal peace on earth is available through Christ!

---

[1]Jane Fritsch, "Rescue Workers Rush In, but Many Do Not Return," *New York Times,* 12 September, 2001, p. 2.

[2]C. F. Keil, *Commentary on the Old Testament in Ten Volumes* (Grand Rapids: William Eerdmans Publishing Company), p. 419.

[3]John Walvoord and Roy Zuck, eds., *The Bible Knowledge Commentary,* vol. 1 (Victor Books, 1987), p. 1478.

[4]Keil, p. 427.

[5]Mark Rizzo, *Criminal Justice Chaplaincy Training Manual.*

[6]N. R. Kleinfeld, "A Creeping Horror: Buildings Burn and Fall As Onlookers Search for Elusive Safety," *New York Times,* 12 September, 2001, p. 1.

[7]N. R. Kleinfeld, "A City of Quiet: Nothing Is the Same One Day After," *New York Times,* 13 September, 2001, p. 1.

CHAPTER 6

The Savior and the City

The phone rang early one morning. Gladys's calm voice was quiet yet full of sorrow. She got right to the point: "Jerry was run over in a hit-and-run accident last night as he walked across the street. Could you come over and tell Kenny what has happened?"

Jerry and Gladys, a Black American couple, began attending our church when they received a vacation Bible school flier on their door. They wanted a safe spiritual harbor for their grandson Kenny, so they visited our service on a Sunday morning. I remember vividly their first visit. As I asked visitors to stand and tell us how they found out about our church, Gladys stood and sternly said, "I would like to know why you are here." A silence fell over our service. Gladys clearly wanted to know why a white man had come into a middle-class, 80 percent Black American community to start a church. I appreciated her honesty and frankness! Perhaps she asked what many thought but feared to verbalize.

I was on the spot, and I answered carefully from Scripture: "Jesus entered the city of Samaria and because the Samaritans had no dealing with the Jews, the woman of Samaria wanted to know why He would ask her for a drink. Jesus replied that 'If thou knewest the gift of God, and who it is that saith to thee, Give me to drink; thou wouldest have asked of him, and he would have given thee living water' (John 4:10). We are here to share the gift of God, which is eternal life, with people." My response disarmed her, and I could sense the congregation, comprised of Black Americans, West Indians, and Filipinos, breathe a sigh of relief.

I could not believe that Jerry was now dead. I had seen him the night before when he picked up Kenny, his eight-year-old grandson, from our weekly Tuesday afternoon Bible Club. His last words to me were "If Gladys or I can do anything to help you, please let us know. We love all that you and Debbie do for us." Gladys and Jerry were raising their grandson, and Jerry was a friend and a father for Kenny. They were also our friends, and they encouraged our church and my family in so many ways.

I went over to see Gladys and she woke up Kenny. I entered his room and told him the news. We cried and prayed together. I felt a great sense of helplessness as I did my best to reach out to this dear family at a time of sudden loss. That day made me realize that the people who have hurts and sorrows in our cities today are not different from those who suffered in Jesus' day.

From the start of His earthly ministry in the city of Nazareth in Luke 4 to His atoning death on Calvary's cross outside the city of Jerusalem, Jesus Christ intimately involved Himself with city work. His message in the city of Nazareth incited the violence of the people with whom He grew up. They rose up with wrath and screamed shouts of death as they "thrust him out of the city" (Luke 4:29). Jesus was thrust out of his own hometown! In the silence of sadness, Jesus allowed them to push Him out of His beloved Nazareth all the way to a cliff that they might brutally cast Him down headfirst. Standing on the brink of that hill, Jesus demonstrated sovereign strength and control as He stopped, passed through the midst of them, and "went his way" (Luke 4:30). What a picture of God's ways! God allows man to willfully reject His Word and His love, but God allows man to go only so far. Ultimately, God will have "his way."

Thrust out of one city, Jesus was not cast down. He continued ministry in the city without discouragement. He entered directly into the city of Capernaum and preached there. At that point, Jesus stated a foundational principle of his earthly ministry when He said, "I must preach the kingdom of God to other cities also: for therefore am I sent" (Luke 4:43).

In 1858 a citywide revival swept the city of Philadelphia. Dudly Tyng pastored a large fashionable church in this city, but, like Jesus, his strong preaching against sin caused his cultured congregation to reject him. He left this church and began another church that began to grow. He also started noontime meetings at a YMCA. On Tuesday, March 30, 1858, over five thousand heard him preach a sermon entitled "Go now ye that are men, and serve the Lord" (Exodus 10:11). Over a thousand men responded at the invitation to commit their hearts and lives to Christ. He said on that occasion, "I must tell my Master's message and I would rather that this right arm be amputated than to come short of my duty in delivering God's message to you." The following Wednesday, in an accident, his right arm was pulled into a farm machine. It became obvious he would not recover from the shock and loss of blood. Before Dudly Tyng would enter God's presence, however, he whispered these words from his hospital bed: "Stand up for Jesus." These were the words that inflamed George Duffield to pen the song with this title. Today we need to stand up for Jesus in the great urban centers of our world and proclaim the Word of God. Let us also have this principle guiding our life: "I must preach the kingdom of God to other cities also: for therefore am I sent" (Luke 4:43).

As we survey the city work of Jesus Christ, let us look at three different cities and three different souls whose needs He met. Luke seeks to get our attention to behold the people of the city who received grace from our Lord Jesus Christ.

BEHOLD A DESPISED CITY LEPER

In an unnamed city, Jesus met a despised city leper. "And it came to pass, when he was in a certain *city, behold* a man full of leprosy: who seeing Jesus fell on his face, and besought him, saying, Lord, if thou wilt, thou canst make me clean. And he put forth his hand, and touched him, saying, I will: be thou clean. And immediately the leprosy departed from him" (Luke 5:12-13). I can see this leper with disheveled hair, tattered clothes, and a soiled covering upon his upper lip. Dirt mingled with sweat and puss covered the rotten rags over his body full of leprosy. The rabbis and doctors of Jesus' day possessed no cure for leprosy. Rather, a rabbi boasted "that he threw stones at them to keep them far off, while others hid themselves or ran away."[1] Religion in Jesus' day not only demonstrated powerlessness to deal with this leper's plight; but it also behaved with hypocritical cruelty. Sin makes a person odious and difficult to love. Religion holds no cure. Is there any hope for someone like this? Have you ever smelled the breath of a drunkard? Have you ever spoken to a crazed homeless person? God must guard us from stuffy religion that looks down our Fundamentalist noses at people completely full of sin. Cruel and feeble religion is not the faith of God's true children. Our faith in Christ leads us to the need; we do not pass by on "the other side" of the road (Luke 10:31-32). Religion asks, "What will happen to me if I try to help this man?" Real faith asks, "What will be his destiny if I do not try to arrest him with the gospel of grace?"

Police cars in New York City contain the three letters CPR. An ambulance crew uses CPR, or cardiopulmonary resuscitation, to breathe life into a victim struggling for breath. The police CPR reminds us that they are ministers of God who labor with "Courtesy, Professionalism, and Respect." A similar attitude of respect for human life should exist in our hearts for all bearers of the image of God as we ask God to use us to give spiritual CPR to lost souls through God's life-giving Word.

Jesus was unlike the religious rabbis. This leper sensed a welcoming spirit from the Savior; he came humbly and helplessly before the Great Physician. Accustomed to running from a religious man, this man with his filthy rags came to Christ, who had laid aside His regal robes in heaven to clothe Himself with flesh for this very purpose—to touch such hopeful hopeless sinners. All of us at one time thought we were hopeless. Nevertheless, when we came to Christ, we came with hope. Against hope he believed in hope as in faith he cried, "Lord, if thou wilt, thou canst make me clean." This man had faith in the divine person and power of Jesus Christ. The word "canst" is *dunamai,* a word often translated "power" or "miracle." He believed in His heart that Jesus was Lord and had the ability in Himself to make him clean. The law said he was to "put a covering upon his upper lip" and cry, "Unclean, unclean" (Leviticus 13:45). When he met Jesus, this leper did not cry "unclean" because He knew Jesus could make him clean. This leper also showed great hope in entering into the city, for lepers were to "dwell alone" and "without the camp" (Leviticus 13:46). True to His Word, Jesus did not cast him out, for Jesus came "to seek and to save that which was lost" (Luke 19:10). Jesus performed the amazing. He touched the untouchable, He cured the incurable, and He loved the unlovable. No one is broken beyond repair if he believes and comes to the Lord Jesus Christ.

If God is going to use us in the city today, we must also do the unthinkable. We must touch the untouchable, love the unlovable, and by God's grace we can see the incurable cured. Thousands roam the urban jungles with oozing spiritual sores and deep emotional hurt. Their only hope is the divine touch of the Great Physician.

I sat in the subway waiting for the doors to close when the lights went out. I was returning home after a rock music concert at Central Park. I was not a Christian at the time. When the lights went out in the Columbus Circle subway station, I did not realize the extent of gloom. I made my way back up to the street and darkness shrouded the night; the whole city had indeed experienced a blackout. To see this city of bright lights in this condition amazed me. I squeezed onto a bus going uptown. The vehicle filled quickly with straphangers. At each stop, more people frantically tried to push their way onto a bus already packed to the limit. I could see panic in the eyes of those left behind as the bus doors closed. As I made my way uptown to the bus terminal by the George Washington Bridge, I heard of robbery and looting throughout the city. During the next couple of days there would be over one billion dollars in damage caused by human greed and evil. Some called that night in July of 1977 "the night of terror." Appliance stores, gift shops, clothing stores, and grocery stores were robbed; shelves were emptied bare by thieves. Without the light, sin came to the surface and spread like leprosy. The people loved the darkness rather than the light, and the blackout demonstrated their sinful, depraved condition. New York City sometimes reminds me of a leper, but we need to love this city and others that often seem unlovable. We need to touch cities that often seem untouchable. We need to pray that our cities with oozing sores will be healed by the power of Jesus Christ!

BEHOLD A DEAD CITY SON

In the city of Nain Jesus met a dead city son and his despondent mother. "Now when he came nigh to the gate of the *city, behold,* there was a dead man carried out, the only son of his mother, and she was a widow: and much people of the city was with her" (Luke 7:12). Luke now confronts us with death and discouragement.

We see in this city *great grief.* Not only was a grief-stricken mother burying her son but also a lonely widow was mourning the untimely loss of her only son. At Jewish funerals, flutes, cymbals, and trumpets played a mournful dirge. Friends who carried the coffin were relieved and replaced. During these intervals, loud shouts of lamentation filled the air as professional mourners cried.

In the midst of this grief the Lord of life came to provide *great grace.* As Jesus saw this heavy-hearted funeral procession and this widow in need, "he had compassion on her, and said unto her, Weep not." Jesus' compassion "approximates the moral equivalent of a physical cardiac arrest."[2]

Learn this vital lesson for urban ministry: in the city we must have compassion, the badge of credibility. Our message and life will have credibility when others see compassion rather than complacency. The sight of the widow moved Jesus' inner being. In compassion He spoke: "Weep not." His words prepared this mother for a mighty miracle. In his earthly life, Jesus never met a funeral without putting it to death! Then Jesus in tenderness touched the unclean coffin. There is practical action behind real compassion. Finally, Jesus spoke again, this time to the dead. Jesus communicated, with the power to raise the dead. This is missions! His command conquered death. "Young man, I say unto thee, Arise" (Luke 7:14). I remember Irish pastor Ian Paisley praying once, "Lord, speak with the voice that raises the dead!" His Word still penetrates souls dead in trespasses and in sins and raises them to life.

The manifestation of the grace of our Lord resulted in *great gladness.* That crowd of mourners turned into a multitude of victors as the young man sat up on the funeral bier and "began to speak" (Luke 7:15). When the Lord gives life to one dead, there are definite evidences of the reality of life. One indication that one dead in sin now lives is that he speaks. New converts must be taught to speak to God in prayer and to speak for God as a witness. Another wonderful truth in this narrative is that Jesus "delivered him [the son once dead] to his mother." Jesus seeks to restore broken relationships in families that have experienced crushing sorrow. "And there came a fear on all: and they glorified God, saying, That a great prophet is risen up among us; and, That God hath visited his people" (Luke 7:16).

Our urban centers are full of widowed mothers who sorrow over the death of their children. We need Jesus' gracious compassion to move us to action. Real compassion cannot leave us immobile. At one time in our church we had five mothers who had sons who had been murdered in cold blood. These mothers needed the comfort found only in the Word of God, and it brought my heart great joy and satisfaction ministering to hearts so hungry to hear from God and His Word. Our cities are also full of youth hardened and toughened by the concrete streets. Many know nothing but hatred and rejection. One teen shot and killed a man yet coldly stated, "It wasn't nothing. I didn't think twice about it. If I had to kill him, I had to kill him. That's the way I look at it cause I'm young. The most I could've gotten was eighteen months." City youth often seek out gangs in order to find security and acceptance. When home and school do not work out, they look to each other for islands of safety and a sense of belonging. The Lord of life still rules and reigns to bring His grace and gladness to the city where grief seems to prevail.

BEHOLD A DEFILED CITY WOMAN

In another city Jesus met a defiled city woman. "And *behold,* a woman in the *city,* which was a sinner, when she knew that Jesus sat at meat in the Pharisee's house, brought an alabaster box of ointment" (Luke 7:37). Luke beckons us now to gaze upon a woman "which was a sinner" but is now a saint. The overwhelming love of God makes whole a prostitute. I see three simple secrets revealed by the life of this saved sinner.

This woman gives to us the secret of how God can effect *significant change* in the direction of a life. The secret to lasting change is repentance at the feet of Jesus. Repentance is a change of mind as a gift of God on account of God's goodness. Real repentance is accompanied by a sorrow for sin and a saving faith in Jesus Christ (Acts 3:19; Acts 20:21; II Corinthians 7:9; Romans 2:4). This woman realized God was good, she was deeply convicted over her sin, and she mourned deeply over her sin. She came to the feet of Jesus to lay down her burden and find the blessing of eternal life. Ministry that does not teach the vital importance of repentance will not see lasting change in lives. Many misunderstand repentance today, both inside and outside the church. The fact remains that repentance is a truth that gives us hope that change is possible by the grace of God.

This nameless woman also gives to us the secret of *loving God* much. This woman with a flaming heart of appreciation to God shows us that in the city there is great potential to see souls forgiven and to see them fall in love with Christ. What makes certain Christians love their Savior so much, and other Christians go through the motions of empty service? Who will love Jesus much? Jesus tells us that it is the one who has been forgiven much. "Her sins, which are many, are forgiven; for she loved much: but to whom little is forgiven, the same loveth little" (Luke 7:47). Our love for God never earns forgiveness, but the measure of our love for God proves forgiveness. The greatness of our sin against God lies not so much in the acts committed as in the greatness of the Person we have sinned against. Although sinners saved out of wretched backgrounds sometimes shine the brightest for our Lord, for they have a deep consciousness of their sin, all must come to the realization that we have sinned greatly against God. Simon the religious Pharisee lacked the essence of true religion, which is a love relationship with God. He never grasped the amazing grace of God's forgiveness. The woman of the city, however, entered into the forgiveness of Jesus and challenges us to never get over the grace of God in forgiving us of our sin. Our love for God will be in direct proportion to our realization that we have been forgiven much by Him.

The third secret we learn from this woman is the secret of *real peace*. The secret of peace in the soul is discovered through the assurance of salvation. Jesus gave this woman His word of assurance that granted her peace: "Thy faith hath saved thee; go in peace" (Luke 7:50). Teaching assurance of salvation is one of the first things a disciple maker must do for a new convert.

Jesus also gave assurance to the paralytic man he healed at the pool of Bethesda. Jesus "said unto him, Behold, thou art made whole: sin no more, lest a worse thing come unto thee." The phrase "behold, thou art made whole" emphasizes to this man that what had taken place in his heart and body was real. This gave him assurance in the reality of God's work in his life. I seek to teach young converts very early in their spiritual life the fact of assurance of salvation. This is the secret of going with God's peace that passes all understanding.

In each of these three passages we find two key words: "behold" and "city." These narratives live on, for they encourage us to behold the city today. People all around us are just like the despised leper, the dead young man, the despondent mother, and the defiled woman. As a young believer, I met a vibrant Christian named Joe. Before his conversion, Joe had lived a selfish life of sin and heroin addiction. One night he went to jump off the George Washington Bridge to end his life. He walked to the middle of this massive structure connecting New York City to New Jersey, but he could not bring himself to terminate his earthly life. He felt like an abject failure. Not long after this, he walked through a park in upper Manhattan. He asked himself the question "Who is God?" As he looked down in despair, he saw a brief phrase scratched in the ground with a stick: "God is love." Soon after this he came to the Lord of love and served our Savior with a heart of appreciation.

Beholding the multitudes in the city reminds me of the story of a little boy on a beach in Australia. I have heard it told that each year thousands of starfish are washed up on the sand in Australia. Usually at night, at high tide, a large wave will bring them in so far that the water will not carry them back out. Then, as the sun shines on the starfish, they slowly dry out and die. One morning a tourist came out of his hotel for a jog. On the beach he noticed a little boy picking up stranded starfish and throwing them back into the sea. There were thousands of them up and down the shore. The man ran up to the boy and said, "I know what you're doing and I think I know why you are doing it. But there are thousands of starfish here and miles and miles of beach. Do you really think that what you are doing is going to make a difference?" The boy said, "I don't know but I think it will make a difference to this one." He picked up another starfish and threw it into the sea. The ministry is like that. We must behold the city one soul at a time, having the kind of compassion that makes a difference on the souls we touch.

---

[1] Alfred Edersheim, *The Life and Times of Jesus the Messiah* (McLean, Va.: MacDonald Publishing Company, 1886), p. 495.

[2] Douglas McLachlan, *Reclaiming Authentic Fundamentalism* (Independence, Mo.: American Association of Christian Schools, 1993), p. 74.

CHAPTER 7

Great Joy in the City

The Book of Acts is a manual for urban church planting. Jesus told the disciples "that they should not depart from Jerusalem, but wait for the promise of the Father" (Acts 1:4). This speaks of the coming in power of the Holy Spirit on the Day of Pentecost. This forceful command coupled with a promise by Jesus directed the disciples to stay in Jerusalem because otherwise they would have wanted to return to their homes in Galilee. "But ye shall receive power, after that the Holy Ghost is come upon you: and ye shall be witnesses unto me both in Jerusalem, and in all Judaea, and in Samaria, and unto the uttermost part of the earth" (Acts 1:8).

I have often heard people liken the reaching of Jerusalem in this verse to reaching our hometown first. Have you seen bulletin boards that compare Jerusalem to your hometown, Judaea to your home state, Samaria to neighboring states or nations, and the uttermost part of the world to somewhere across the ocean? I have seen many of these through the years, and I must disagree with this interpretation of Acts 1:8. Although I agree that we must fervently witness where we live, Jesus did not tell His disciples to reach their hometown first; otherwise, He would have told them to go home to Galilee! Jerusalem was not the hometown of the disciples. Jesus told them to wait in Jerusalem.

Reaching our Jerusalem is remaining in the capital cities of our nations, cities vehemently opposed to the gospel of Christ. Jerusalem was the lions' den of animosity toward anyone associated with Jesus of Nazareth. Reaching our Jerusalem first speaks of staying in the cultural, religious, and commercial center of our nation that is most opposed to our message and ministry and preaching Christ in the power of the Holy Spirit. Acts 1:8 challenges us to reach the city in order to influence the country.

Acts 8 begins the third stage of the early church's witness for Christ. The disciples were to be witnesses in Jerusalem and then Judaea and then Samaria. The gospel was for "the Jew first, and also to the Greek" (Romans 1:16). That is, the primary need of the Jew or the Greek is the gospel. The disciples "filled Jerusalem" with the doctrine of Christ (Acts 5:28). That ought to be the goal of any church in any city! The gospel then penetrated the surrounding area called Judaea. As the gospel moved from the Jewish area of Jerusalem and Judaea into the half-Jewish region of Samaria, the gospel broke first into the city of Samaria. The gospel penetrated the city and then affected the surrounding areas. The city was center stage as the gospel spread to the uttermost part of the earth. Paul also went to the major cities of his day: Philippi, Thessalonica, Athens, Corinth, Ephesus, and finally Rome. As we read of the establishment and expansion of the early church, we can see that New Testament missions was primarily urban church planting. This does not mean that reaching rural areas is not important. Every soul without Christ has eternal value; every little village without the gospel needs a missionary. However, reaching the cities ought to be the priority and primary thrust of our missionary, church planting, and evangelistic endeavors.

The odds of great joy coming to the city of Samaria were slim to none. Everything seemed to be against anything good happening in Samaria, yet "there was great joy in that city" (Acts 8:8). Real joy is not realized through government programs or the election of favored politicians. Joy is a fruit of the Spirit based on a personal faith relationship with God through His Son Jesus Christ, which produces inner strength, confidence, and power for living. God alone can cultivate this kind of joy. Let us see some things about the great joy in the city of Samaria.

GREAT JOY OUT OF GREAT TRIAL

Great joy came out of the great trial of persecution. In Acts 8:1 we find the second mention of Saul in the New Testament. The first mention occurs in Acts 7:58, when Saul supervised and took pleasure in the stoning of Stephen. What an introduction to this man who would turn the world upside down for Christ and become a great urban missionary! Saul consented to the death of Stephen, and then "made havock of the church" (Acts 8:3). He sought its destruction. He ravaged it; he burned it to the ground. He behaved like a wild animal tearing up its victim; he raged like a crazed bull against the very Lord who had died for him, kicking against the pricks. Saul was a pioneer persecutor of the church. To destroy the church was not an easy task, for it was not just a building in Jerusalem that had to be demolished. The church consisted of people, and the people met in homes. Saul entered into the homes of believers, both men and women, unnamed heroes of the faith, and dragged them in front of the Sanhedrin to commit them to prison. Even before he was saved, Saul unwittingly contributed to the spread of the church, for this persecution led to the scattering of the believers like seeds across the land. This persecution actually led to the establishing of the church in Antioch that he later joined and from which he was sent (Acts 11:19-20)!

The great joy also came out of the trial of great lamentation over the death of Stephen (Acts 8:2). Stephen's martyrdom precipitated even greater persecution against the growing church. His death increased the confidence of the persecutors. Stephen was a good man and full of the Holy Ghost. He was one of the first deacons chosen by the church (Acts 6:5).

The great joy came out of the trial of a great scattering of the church (Acts 8:1, 4). All the believers except the apostles were forced to scatter. Since we naturally cling to our homes, leaving is a great trial. The "normal believer" was scattered and went everywhere preaching the Word. It was the "average Joe," the "common Christian," who realized the responsibility to be a witness of the Resurrection. The persecution acted like wind to a seed, for it spread the church across the world. People are looking for something to live for; when you are willing to die for something, that is something to live for!

GREAT JOY DESPITE GREAT OBSTACLES

Samaria was not a paradise for a Jew like Philip. This was a place where one would have said, "No Jew can have a successful ministry there!" Samaria threatened Philip's comfort zone as cities today will challenge the comfort level of anyone desiring to live a godly life for Jesus Christ. Yet the Lord commissioned him to go there and preach the Word of God as a witness of the Resurrection.

The first obstacle was racial prejudice. Samaritans were *hostile* to the Jews. Hundreds of years of conflict had led to great resentment between Judaea and Samaria. Samaria became the capital of the Northern Kingdom of Israel and was a powerful idolatrous center when Ahab and Jezebel ruled (I Kings 16:29-33). The introduction of Jezebel's Baal religion into Israel, coupled with Jeroboam's counterfeit Judaism, ultimately led to the captivity of the Northern Kingdom in 722 B.C. by Assyria. After captivity, Samaria became a mixed area of Gentile and Jew. The Jews who remained in the land intermarried with Gentiles and lost their racial distinctiveness as well as the true worship of the God of Abraham, Isaac, and Jacob. Alexander the Great took the city in 331 B.C. and introduced Greek culture. In 128 B.C. a Jewish zealot named John Hyrcanus destroyed the temple in Samaria upon Mt. Gerizim, increasing tensions even more. For these reasons, in New Testament times, Jews had "no dealings with the Samaritans" (John 4:9).

One thing we must remember is that Jesus prepared the way for Philip's ministry. Jesus Himself went into Samaria, and some believed in Him just a few years before Philip came to preach Christ. During Jesus' memorable conversation with the woman at the well (John 4), many left the city and "came unto him" (John 4:30). When we enter into a city with great need, we can be assured that the Lord has gone before us and prepared hearts to hear His Word.

Even in the most hostile places, Jesus prepares the way for ministry. Many Bible Christians avoid cities today because of a lack of comfort with different cultures. The lack of cultural diversity among Fundamentalist churches today is alarming and should shock us into change. Of all people, those who name Christ should make no racial preference. Because we have one God, there ought to be no barriers. Our God is the Creator of all men. We have come from the same parents twice over; we came from Adam and Eve at Creation, and we came from Noah and his wife after the destruction of the world. Most importantly, we have a Savior who commissioned twelve Jewish apostles to go into the world and reach every ethnic group!

The second obstacle was the immoral living of the Samaritans; they were a *carnal* people. Do you remember Jesus' ministry in Samaria when He met the woman who had been married five times? The man she was living with when she met Jesus was not even her husband, yet she had a religious hope. This sounds like some modern American city!

The city is full of broken homes with people who have given up on God's blueprint for the family. People indulge their flesh yet maintain some religious profession. Can the message of Jesus Christ be received in a city where men's desires are so sensual? Can the message of Jesus Christ be received in a city where people take pride in their indecency? Yes, for the gospel of Christ "is the power of God unto salvation to everyone that believeth; to the Jew first, and also to the Greek."

The third obstacle was false religion. Samaritans were *religious but lost.* Recall that the Samaritan woman had a messianic hope, yet she was lost until she met Jesus. Religion has never saved anyone; religion is often the greatest enemy of the true gospel. Never think that the city is not a place full of religion. There is no shortage of religion in major cities such as New York City, where over five thousand churches own property valued at five billion dollars! New York City is a stronghold of Roman Catholicism (2.4 million, or 30 percent of the population), a bastion for the Jewish community (1.7 million with the strict Hasidic groups as well), and a place where cults thrive and flourish. New York City is home to the world headquarters of the Jehovah's Witnesses as well as the dwelling of four of the top ten religious magazines in our nation (including *Guideposts, Awake,* and *Watchtower*). More than three hundred national and international religious groups have their main offices in New York City. With this great plethora of religion, there is nevertheless a great shortage of true faith. Like the Samaritan woman, many in our cities are religious but lost.

GREAT JOY THROUGH ONE GREAT SERVANT

Philip, scattered and forced to leave his home, remembered his calling and the purpose of his salvation. He was one of the seven deacons chosen along with Stephen. He was a man who stood out and stood up for his Lord. He did not care what people thought of him.

We once had a group of young men from a Christian college visit our church. While they stayed in our home, they shared their testimonies during our family devotions. Two of them said they had gone to Christian schools yet stood out as the oddballs at their school because they were surrendered to the Lord to preach the Word of God. If they stood out as somewhat strange in a Christian setting, how much more will we be considered a "peculiar people" in a city hostile to the Word of God? Yes, people will think it strange that we do not run with them in their "same excess of riot" (I Peter 4:4), but we are following the footsteps of Jesus. I am sure that Philip was considered an oddball by many, for he was full of the Holy Spirit and of faith.

Never think that one man cannot have a great influence. It is usually one person who does great things. Never think, "It is only me, I cannot do it alone." J. Oswald Sanders, in his classic work *Spiritual Leadership,* shared this poem by George Liddell:

Give me a man of God—one man,
Whose faith is master of his mind,
And I will right all wrongs
And bless the name of all mankind.

Give me a man of God—one man,
Whose tongue is touched with heaven's fire,
And I will flame the darkest hearts
With high resolve and deep desire.

Give me a man of God—one man,
One mighty prophet of the Lord,
And I will give you peace on earth,
Bought with a prayer and not a sword.

Give me a man of God—one man,
True to the vision that he sees,
And I will build your broken shrines
And bring the nations to their knees.[1]

It was to Ezekiel that God said, "And I sought for a man among them, that should make up the hedge, and stand in the gap before me for the land, that I should not destroy it: but I found none" (Ezekiel 22:30). It was to Jesus that the lame man said, "I have no man . . . to put me into the pool" (John 5:7). It was David who cried to God in his overwhelmed state: "I looked on my right hand, and beheld, but there was no man that would know me: refuge failed me; no man cared for my soul" (Psalm 142:4). It was one man who inspired millions when he said, "I have a dream." It was one man who said: "Mr. Gorbachov, tear down this wall." It was one man who said, "We have nothing to fear but fear itself." God is looking for one man who will rise up, serve Him, help others, do His will, and stand for Him in places others fear to go.

On Fourteenth Street in Manhattan, this statement by General William Booth, founder of the Salvation Army, can be found on the outside of the Salvation Army building:

> While women weep as they do now, I'll fight. While men go to prison, in and out, in and out, as they do now, I'll fight. Where there is a drunkard left; while there is a poor lost girl upon the streets; while there remains one dark soul, without the life of God; I'll fight! I'll fight to the very end!

It takes only one man to stand up and fight to serve God. You never know; the result could be "great joy in that city."

GREAT JOY THROUGH GREAT PREACHING

Never underestimate the wonder of preaching. It is through preaching that men and women hear of the salvation through Jesus Christ. How shall they hear without a preacher? It is through the foolishness of preaching that people are saved. God has not called us to protests, parades, or photo-ops, but to preach the Word. We are not commanded to get media attention or to stop traffic in the middle of Broadway and Forty-second Street. We are commanded to preach the Word. In Acts 8:4, the phrase "preaching the word" means that the church evangelized, preaching the good news. Jesus is the Word of God (John 1:1). This phrase emphasizes the authority of our message. We have a message that still brings great joy to all people (Luke 2:10). Jesus Christ is the life who can make complete the shattered urban life.

In Acts 8:5 we read that Philip "preached Christ unto them." The word "preached" here means they authoritatively proclaimed the Christ. It emphasizes the authority of the messenger, for we are ambassadors for Christ. As His emissaries we are authoritatively commissioned by Him to go into all the world. As Philip "preached Christ unto them," the people listened. Preaching God's Word brings the presence of Jesus Christ to people. The presence of Jesus Christ brings fullness of joy; this is the strength and power by which we live. Philip did not present theory, opinion, or speculation, but the person and work of Jesus Christ. Who is Jesus? He is the God-Man. He is one person, yet He possesses two distinct natures, human and divine. What did He do? He lived a righteous life, He died and shed His blood for the sins of the world, He rose again, He ascended into heaven, He intercedes for us today, and He is coming again.

Preaching takes blood, sweat, tears, and a lot of time. As feeding people a good meal satisfies the one who prepares it as well as the one who eats it, so preparing a biblical message through prayer and study brings joy as it feeds both preacher and hearer. We must work hard to see visitors come to church. We must work harder to feed them God's truth when they come so that they will come back. As hard as it is to get someone to come the first time to church, it is harder to get them to come back. We preach God's Word to glorify God and see lives transformed into His image.

Before we witness to someone, we need to be sure we can state our message in a sentence. We need to communicate clear points based on eternal truth. Our messages ought to be Christ-centered, contextually accurate, practical, timeless, and clear. It is better to be clear than cute! In delivering the message, we need to be filled with the Spirit, personal, honest, and compassionate. Ask God to take away harshness; we are not persuasive when we are abrasive. "The sweetness of the lips increaseth learning" and "pleasant words are as an honeycomb, sweet to the soul, and health to the bones" (Proverbs 16:21, 24). "Speaking the truth in love" helps the hearer to "grow up into him in all things" (Ephesians 4:15).

God did a miraculous work in Samaria through Philip's ministry: "And the people with one accord gave heed unto those things which Philip spake, hearing and seeing the miracles which he did. For unclean spirits, crying with loud voice, came out of many that were possessed with them: and many taken with palsies, and that were lame, were healed" (Acts 8:6-7). Sometimes we read of these mighty miracles taking place, and we think this phenomenon is still needed if we are going to see people believe.

Remember two things about the miracles of the early church. First, this young church did not have one verse of the New Testament. The miracles authenticated the gospel message before the completion of the New Testament. Second, miracles did not keep the enemies of God from waging a massive war against the early church. The miracles Jesus worked did not lead people with blind eyes to believe (John 12:37-41). The emphasis in Acts 8 is upon the preaching of the Word and the proclaiming of Jesus Christ. The miracles confirmed the message; they authenticated the accuracy of what they said about Jesus Christ. The people gave heed to the word because of the miracles, but it was not the miracles themselves that brought the joy.

GREAT JOY THROUGH GREAT LIFE TRANSFORMATIONS

Yes, the transformation of lives leads to great joy. How can the multitudes be transformed? God transforms people one soul at a time. We must never be discouraged, brethren. The Lord is at work in our lives, changing us into His image.

When people are saved, great joy occurs in the city. When saved people are changed into the image of Jesus, great joy comes to the city. Do you not hunger for this kind of joy in your city? Not the passing pleasure of some ticker-tape parade, but the surpassing joy of being used of God to see lives transformed. When the Yankees win the pennant, there is joy in the city for a while, but when lives are saved and delivered from the bondage of sin, joy arrives that remains! When a soul has thoughts of sin and suicide but then is converted and given a reason for living, there will be great joy in that heart and in that home. When a man curses and beats his wife or children but repents of his behavior and finds grace to love, there will be great joy in that heart and in that home. When one has heavy credit card debt and the burdens have caused the joy to cease, and that one who was before out of control finds true riches in Christ, there will be great joy in that heart and in that home. When one is under the influence of demons, with paranoia, temptation, and loss of sleep, and the power of Jesus frees him from those unclean spirits, there will be great joy in that heart and in that home.

When enough hearts and homes receive the joy of the Lord, then the city will be set to rejoice as well. Jesus Christ can put to death the killjoys of joy: selfishness, bitterness, anger, and fear. Jesus Christ changes a person from being a taker to being a giver, and giving people are joyful. Jesus Christ changes a person from being bitter to being forgiving, and forgiving people are joyful. Jesus Christ changes a person from fearing to rejoicing in His presence. Jesus changes a person from focusing on problems to focusing on His power. When souls are delivered from physical sickness, great joy occurs. When souls are delivered from demonic power, great joy results. Praise God that He does deliver souls from disease and demons! Do you know that coming to Jesus can save from much physical danger—from HIV, from cirrhosis of the liver, from lung cancer, and even from the headaches caused by stress? Jesus can deliver a soul from adultery and fornication, from pornography and abusive behavior. He can deliver a soul from homosexuality and drunkenness, from drug usage and anger. Jesus can deliver us from all types and manner of sin. The gospel does not leave us where we were. God loves souls right where they are, but He loves them too much to let them stay that way. The God of the gospel has the power to convict and change "whosoever shall confess that Jesus is the Son of God" (I John 4:15). The gospel of Jesus washes, cleanses, justifies, and sanctifies without respect of persons all who call upon the name of the Lord.

In 1958, at the age of fourteen, Karen ran away from home. That journey led her first to a children's shelter, then to a juvenile detention center, and at the age of sixteen, into a prison. At the age of nineteen, after finishing her prison sentence, Karen was introduced to heroin by a girl she had met in prison. Here is the rest of her story in her own words.

"I supported my habit the following years by prostitution, shoplifting, forgery, burglary, and selling drugs. I then began drinking. All I did was exchange one drug for another. In my twisted reasoning, I thought it was better to be called an 'alcoholic' than an 'addict.' There was an enormous void in my life, and I was aware of it, so I tried to fill it with either drugs or drink. In 1979, I met my husband and I got a good job with the Transit Authority. I was making good money and had a good life, but still I drank. In 1990, unbeknownst to my husband, I started using cocaine. In 1994 we were divorced and I walked away from my job. Soon after, I was arrested for selling drugs. While in my cell that first night, I got down on my knees and prayed for the first time in many years. The prayer I prayed was a 'foxhole prayer,' for no sooner did God answer it than I was back on the streets drinking and doing drugs. I wound up homeless for a year and a half. I literally slept on benches in the park or cardboard on the sidewalks. I always had a bottle by my side. I wanted to stop but I couldn't. Addiction was what I had known from the age of nineteen until I was fifty-two. There was never a day I was not high on something unless I was in a detoxification center or prison. While homeless, different groups would come to us and witness and pray with us. When they stood holding my hand praying for me, I would be overcome and begin crying. The Lord was convicting me although I did not know it at the time. As soon as they left, I would pick up my bottle. At the end of my day panhandling, I would go to a Catholic church and put my pennies in the poor box. Then I would get on my knees and cry while I prayed. I can see now that some of it was prayer but most of it was self-pity. I had no idea what to do, what to say, or who God really was. God is faithful and He knows our heart, and He knew I needed to be led by the hand, so He sent someone named Glenna to me. She lived in the neighborhood and at times she would come by with food or clothing for us. She never preached but she did show love. She talked about being saved and she left an open invitation for us to accompany her to church. She led me to Jesus in the summer of 1995 and I was baptized a month later. I was still drinking, but I continued to go to church with her, even with alcohol on my breath. I remember the pastor reading from James 1:22 about being 'doers of the word and not hearers only.' I wanted to be a doer, but I could not let go of the bottle. By the winter of 1995, God opened a door for me to get off the street and He gave me a place to stay. I studied the Word and stayed sober for six months, but it was a daily battle. I did not know how to gain the victory through Christ. I was living in my own strength, and the inevitable happened: I started drinking again. I went back to the streets. After about a week of nightly crying to God and thinking I would die with a bottle in my hand, I realized that I had come too far to go out like that! When I went back to church, I felt so hopeless! I remember crying and sobbing out loud to the Lord. I don't think I said anything but His name. I just cried until I thought my chest would break. I know now that was when I truly came to the end of myself. I knew I could not do it by my own power. I understood then what Jesus meant when He said, 'for without me ye can do nothing' (John 15:5). I was truly broken. When I finally stopped shedding tears, I felt like a great weight was lifted off me. I started crying again but this time they were tears of joy and gratitude. I knew the Lord had delivered me from thirty-six years of bondage and addictions. I thank and praise God every day for my salvation and deliverance!"

Karen is now a member of Heritage Baptist Church in Manhattan and has started a homeless ministry in our church to reach people where she used to be. The city of Samaria and Karen's testimony remind us that great joy may come to the city one person at a time. Great joy can still arise out of great trials, despite great obstacles, through one great servant preaching Jesus Christ and through great life transformations. Walk in the Spirit so that you can have the inner strength of God's joy in your life. Work in the power of the Spirit by preaching Christ so that others can learn the joy of a personal faith relationship with God through Jesus Christ. Great joy can come to your city but it begins when great joy abides in your life.

---

[1]Sanders, J. Oswald, *Spiritual Leadership* (Chicago: Moody Press, 1980), p. 17.

CHAPTER 8

Christians First in the City

One must not think that city saints cannot be strong and genuine Christians. The name "Christian" was first used to describe the believers in Antioch, the third largest city in the world during Paul's day. They were called Christians first in Antioch in spite of the plethora of false mystery religions. They were called Christians first in Antioch in spite of the abundance of pagan immorality that infected the culture. Alexander the Great used cities as strategic centers to evangelize the world with Hellenistic culture. For this worldly conqueror, "urbanization became the means of hellenization."[1] The Roman poet Juvenal, writing at the end of the first century A.D., accused Antioch of being the foundation of Rome's perversion.[2] Nevertheless, God did a work in Antioch so that the believers there for the first time were called Christians. Reaching pagan cities like Antioch was not on the agenda of the Jerusalem church, but God had different plans. The believers in Antioch demonstrate that the power of the risen Christ gives strength to be in the city but not of the city. This is because they were Christians first. We must remember that genuine Christianity can thrive in cultures hostile to our message. If inhabitants of Antioch could so energetically live for Christ, so can urban residents today.

Sadly, the name "Christian" does not mean much in our culture. Some use this term to loosely define themselves as something other than Jewish or Muslim. We have lost the very special meaning of the term as it is used in Scripture. In Acts 11:26 we see an amazingly significant statement: "And the disciples were called Christians first in Antioch." This is the first time the word "Christian" appears in Scripture. It occurs in just two other references. King Agrippa said to Paul, "Almost thou persuadest me to be a Christian" (Acts 26:28). The last time this name is used in Scripture is when Peter uses the term to exhort the believers to patient suffering: "Yet if any man suffer as a Christian, let him not be ashamed; but let him glorify God on this behalf" (I Peter 4:16).

Real Christians are genuine disciples and followers of Jesus Christ. The disciples were called Christians because they lived like Jesus Christ. They were called Christians first because they sought Christ first in their lives. They were called Christians not as a result of the culture in Antioch softening toward the things of God. The term "Christian" was given as a title of shame or disgrace to the followers of the Lord Jesus. The context indicates that "it must have been the Gentiles who were listening to their witness who were calling them Christians."[3] Jews would never have used the Greek word for Messiah to name the followers of Jesus. Furthermore, "in the ancient world, slaves were called by their master's name."[4] This name given to shame the followers of Jesus was in fact a badge of honor. The English word "Christ" comes from the Greek word "christos," which means "anointed one." This is synonymous to *"Mashiyach"* in the Hebrew language, which speaks of the Messiah. The term "Christian" refers to those who believed that Jesus is the Messiah. This name of shame, given to believers in the third largest city in the world, characterizes real, genuine followers of Christ in a worldly city. What are the marks of a true Christian and of a genuine Christian church that exists in the heart of urban idolatry? Let us focus on the church of Antioch to see how these believers modeled authentic Christianity.

THEY EVANGELIZE COURAGEOUSLY

The church of Antioch was born out of courageous evangelism that broke with the status quo (which means "the mess we are in"). The persecution that arose after the stoning of Stephen spread the church to Phenice, Cyprus, and Antioch. These believers had strong backbone to endure such persecution. At first, they followed the general pattern of the Jerusalem church; they preached "the word to none but unto the Jews only" (Acts 11:19). As some of the men of Cyprus and Cyrene heard of Christ, believers broke out of their evangelistic narrow-mindedness and started preaching the Lord Jesus "unto the Grecians" (Acts 11:20). "Grecians" is used in the New Testament of Jews born in foreign lands, imitating Greek customs, following pagan religions, and speaking the Greek language.[5] The word also describes Gentiles following the cosmopolitan character of the Greek world. "That was the breakthrough! The earlier preaching of Philip to the Samaritans and the Ethiopian proselyte and Peter's encounter with Cornelius the centurion, remarkable events though they were, still were limited to people within the circle of Jewish faith and piety. But at Antioch pagans heard the gospel from Christian lips, and the universal spread of the Good News began."[6]

The founding of this church demonstrates the courage of the common believer. The "founder" of this congregation remains unknown; his name does not appear in Scripture. In the early church the "average believer" would be considered "above average" in our era. Common Christians had a tremendous sense of ownership in the work of the ministry. They lived what Hudson Taylor said: "It is His work, not mine nor yours, and yet it is ours; not because we are engaged in it, but because we are His and one with Him whose work it is."[7] Too many people have the idea that the church belongs to the pastor. It is "his church." One of my goals as an urban missionary is to daily prove to the people of our church that the church is not "my church." I try not to let others call it "my church" when they are discussing our church just because I am the pastor who happened to be the human instrument in its founding.

These persecuted believers had the courage to preach the Lord Jesus in a simple yet consistent fashion. The persecution they faced did not stop their continued preaching of the good news of Jesus. What an example! Genuine Christians always remember their main work no matter their regular work. The believers in Antioch knew that the preaching of the Lord Jesus was not only for the "pastor." We need to get away from the "Reverend mentality" that permeates our thinking. The key to churches growing in urban melting pots is to get away from the idea of a "paid professional" doing the work. One of the major jobs of an urban church planter is to delegate responsible aspects of the ministry to the common believer. The pastor must equip his people to do the work of the ministry and then trust God to turn them loose. "Ministry takes place when divine resources meet human needs through loving channels to the glory of God."[8] Too many people have the idea that all the work is to be done by the pastor. It is "his work to do." This misconception must consistently be rejected and the truth of Ephesians 4:11-12 taught. Gifted servants are given to the church in order to help believers become mature so that each member can do "the work of the ministry, for the edifying of the body of Christ." As saints are strengthened and brought to spiritual adulthood to do the work of the ministry, the church is built up. Every member is a minister because every believer has access to the resources necessary to be a loving channel for His glory.

THEY ARE STRENGTHENED SUPERNATURALLY

In Acts 11:21 we read that "the hand of the Lord was with them: and a great number believed, and turned unto the Lord." The hand of God speaks of power and direction. The strength that the disciples experienced was strength beyond their ability. Ezra experienced this supernatural strengthening when he said, "I was strengthened as the hand of the Lord my God was upon me" (Ezra 7:28). Nehemiah also knew of this supernatural strength: "Then I told them of the hand of my God which was good upon me" (Nehemiah 2:18). In this church at Antioch, there was no bloated bureaucracy or mere maintenance mentality. There was a dynamic strength from God. The key to this kind of power does not come when people are elected to positions in the church but when they are empowered by God. This was not mere religion at work or a church getting mired in politics, but this was a people enabled by God.

God's empowering of these metropolitan disciples led them to see great growth in the number of believers. "A great number believed, and turned unto the Lord" (Acts 11:21). The hand of God led to people believing and turning to God. This turning is an about-face. It is a conversion that speaks of a dramatic, deliberate, and decisive change. First Thessalonians 1:9 speaks of this kind of conversion: "How ye turned to God from idols to serve the living and true God." Real Christians labor so that men may savingly believe on our Lord Jesus and turn to Him. They know that conversion and the turning of souls to Him is because of the power of His hand.

Do not think that it is a selfish and carnal thing to desire your church to grow and have a great number. Three times in the Acts account we see the numbers or size of the crowd emphasized (vv. 21, 24, 26). Our hearts should hunger to see a great number believe in our Savior. Is this not something for which to labor? Real Christians are strengthened by the hand of God and long and love to see souls turn to the Lord. Real Christians want to see great numbers turn to the Lord! There is nothing spiritual in itself about a small church, a shrinking church, or a dying church. There is nothing necessarily spiritual about a large church either; but if I had my choice, I would rather have a biblical, spiritual growing church, where a great number believe and turn to the Lord, than a church where it is us four and no more. Our heartbeat at Heritage Baptist Church in New York City is that we agree to grow biblically. We dare not compromise biblical doctrine or practice in order to grow. Our church is not a large church, but by God's grace He has increased our church gradually both spiritually and numerically each year. The growth often seems very slow, and the growth is nothing compared to the size of the city and the size of other churches that compromise in areas of doctrine and music. The church is the body of Christ and as the "whole body fitly joined together and compacted by that which every joint supplieth, according to the effectual working in the measure of every part, maketh increase of the body unto the edifying of itself in love" (Ephesians 4:16). The church is built up in love as believers do the work of the ministry. Colossians 2:19 says, "Holding the Head, from which all the body by joints and bands having nourishment ministered, and knit together, increaseth with the increase of God." This church in Antioch increased with the increase that God ordained as His mighty hand provided the strength.

THEY RECEIVE GRACE FREELY

This church experienced the grace of God. Barnabas came to Antioch and "when he came, and had seen the grace of God, was glad, and exhorted them all" (Acts 11:23). I wonder if people visiting in our churches can see the grace of God working in our midst. Grace is God's merciful kindness by which God, doing His drawing work upon souls, turns them to Christ; keeps, strengthens, and increases them in faith, knowledge, and affection; and brings growth in Christian virtues.[9] Grace is God giving people the desire and power to do His will. Grace is God's help! Grace is God's sufficiency that gives His people an attitude of gratitude. We see that grace makes real believers glad. Grace *(charis)* and gladness *(chairo)* go together.

THEY CONTINUE PURPOSEFULLY

Real Christians do not quit. They do not give up serving God. They have resolutely determined and decided to follow Jesus because they have received His grace. They continue because they purpose to abide in the Lord. Barnabas "exhorted [the Antioch believers], that with purpose of heart they would cleave to the Lord." You will never live for the Lord until you purpose to abide in the Lord, His Word, and prayer.

Lieutenant Hiroo Onoda served the Japanese Imperial Army in the Philippines during World War II. He was told that the war would not be short and in the end, Japan would win. "Whatever happens," his commanding officer General Muto said, "We'll come back for you. You may have to live on coconuts. If that's the case, live on coconuts." After the war, Onoda kept to his post. In 1954, he was still at his post along with one other companion. In 1972 his companion was shot while raiding a Filipino village for food. Meanwhile, back in Japan, Onoda had become famous. He was the undefeated samurai! A young Japanese man went out to find Onoda, and Onoda told him, "If you want me to go to Japan, bring me my orders. There must be proper orders!" The young man did that, and finally Onoda was convinced to surrender, thirty years after the war's real conclusion.[10] He was willing to continue in a lost war because he believed what he was told. He had greater commitment to a lost cause than most Christians do to our victorious cause!

THEY SERVE UNSELFISHLY

Barnabas is described as "a good man, and full of the Holy Ghost and of faith: and much people was added unto the Lord" (Act 11:24). In verse 25 we see an obscure verse with major consequences: "Then departed Barnabas to Tarsus, for to seek Saul." What an unselfish Christian he was! Barnabas's unselfish actions cannot be underestimated. This man called the "son of consolation" glorified the Lord by cheerfully seeking Saul in Tarsus. Barnabas was not concerned about building a personal legacy and becoming famous or well known.

The word "to seek" in verse 25 implies that Barnabas had to search for Saul. He had to go up and down in Tarsus, looking for Saul. Why would Barnabas do that? Barnabas knew Saul from his early days in Christ when he came to Jerusalem. Many of the disciples had been afraid of Saul and did not believe his profession of faith, but Barnabas had sought to introduce him and incorporate him into the ministry of the growing Jerusalem church. Perhaps Saul had shared with Barnabas that his calling was to bear the name of Jesus and suffer shame for Him among "the Gentiles, and kings, and the children of Israel" (Acts 9:15).

Others may not have wanted to share the spotlight with someone else, but Barnabas did not minister for his own glory but for the glory of Jesus Christ. Barnabas was not concerned about being number one or number two. What mattered to him was that people were being saved and discipled in order to live for Christ. Saul and Barnabas were not rivals but brothers, fellow soldiers, and co-laborers for their God. It is important in the church that we do not compete with one another, but that we serve our Lord Jesus Christ. Barnabas was secure as a saint in his place in the body of Christ. He was secure with the gifts and abilities God had given him. He was not in competition with anyone else, but he cared only that people were turning to the Lord, and being strengthened to live for God.

We are not in competition. We are to complement one another. We are not to compare our gifts and talents with others, for the comparing business in the church destroys the heart for ministry in the church! We are not adversaries but allies. We are to love one another and to serve the Lord together. We dare not seek after position, but we are to seek after the Lord so that "much people" can be "added unto the Lord" (Acts 11:24*b*).

In this world, we are to serve the Lord. What we do on the surface may be for people. We clothe someone, we feed someone, we counsel someone, or we give someone a drink. If we serve people without realizing that we are serving Jesus Christ, we will burn out, get bitter, and often feel unappreciated. If we serve people realizing that our real service is for the Lord, we will have joy, for we know that He is pleased.

I challenge you to look intensely at your ministry in the church and ask, "How can I serve God in my church? What can I do to function in this body of Christ? How can I take on responsibility and gain ownership in our church?"

We see not only the selflessness of Barnabas but also the unselfishness of this man called Saul. Have you ever felt that perhaps God could not use you? Have you ever felt that you are on a shelf gathering dust? Saul had been dramatically saved (Acts 9:5-6). After his miraculous conversion on the well-known Damascus road, he spent some three years in the Syrian city of Damascus and in Arabia receiving a crash course in Christian theology taught by the Holy Spirit of God (Galatians 1:16-17). Then he went to Jerusalem for a mere fifteen days, speaking boldly in the name of Jesus Christ. During this brief visit, the Grecians sought to kill him (Acts 9:29). In order to spare his life, "the brethren . . . sent him forth to Tarsus," his hometown (Acts 9:30). This begins about eight mysteriously silent years in the life of this amazing man, Saul of Tarsus. What went on in his mind during these eight long years? Did Saul feel like he was on a shelf? Would his past life as a pioneer persecutor threaten his ability to be used in the church of Jesus Christ? There he waited and prepared his heart to serve the Lord. These quiet years of waiting were important years of preparation. In God's sovereignty, as Saul waited upon the Lord renewing his strength in tranquil training in Tarsus, a church was being planted in the great city of Antioch. When Barnabas found Saul, he "brought him unto Antioch. And it came to pass, that a whole year they assembled themselves with the church, and taught much people" (Acts 11:26). When Saul came to Antioch, he did not have a selfish agenda, but he simply desired to fulfill God's purpose for his life: to bear the name of Jesus Christ and suffer shame before the Gentiles, kings, and the children of Israel (Acts 9:15). God's perfect will can come true to those who wait!

THEY GIVE PROPORTIONATELY

This church of Antioch that experienced the grace of God was not only a growing church but also a giving church. They gave in response to a definite need; there was a famine in Jerusalem (Acts 11:27-30). Everyone gave something; everyone gave according to his ability; everyone gave as an act of service. The word "relief" *(diakonia)* means "ministry or service." Some people cannot preach or teach or sing, but they can give. One of the wonderful things about giving is that everyone can get involved because God does not look on the size of the gift but the extent of the sacrifice. "Every man according as he purposeth in his heart, so let him give; not grudgingly, or of necessity: for God loveth a cheerful giver" (II Corinthians 9:7). Giving is a demonstration of sacrificial service to God. Here we see that it is appropriate for a church to be involved in compassionate giving to help relieve suffering and famine.

Not only did this church give generously, but in Acts 13 they also willingly surrendered two key leaders to be "sent away" to begin what many call Paul's first missionary journey. This church puts most of our Fundamentalist churches to shame. They willingly gave two of their most gifted teachers for ministry far from their church. Just as they gave generously toward famine relief in Jerusalem, this church gave generously in fasting, prayer, and ministry unto the Lord. The early church fasted and prayed; we feast and play. A church so devoted to God and focused upon prayer will be a sending church.

This church in Antioch is a model of balance for any church today, but especially the church that exists in the cosmopolitan center of varied cultures. Missionary Dr. Darrell Champlain calls this assembly the "church with a beard" because of their biblical maturity and missionary spirit.

The well-known poem "New Colossus," written by Emma Lazarus on November 2, 1883, is held by Lady Liberty in New York Harbor.

These lines from the poem can remind us of our mission to proclaim a liberty far greater than mere political liberty to the multitudes of immigrants who enter our cities and towns. "Christians first" will flesh out these words in a Christlike spirit:

> *"Give me your tired, your poor,*
> *Your huddled masses yearning to breathe free,*
> *The wretched refuse of your teeming shore.*
> *Send these, the homeless, tempest-tost to me,*
> *I lift my lamp beside the golden door!"*

---

[1]Harvie Conn, "The Kingdom of God and the City of Man: A History of the City/Church Dialogue," in *Discipling the City,* ed. Roger Greenway (Grand Rapids: Baker Book House, 1992), p. 249.

[2]Roger S. Greenway and Timothy M. Monsma, *Cities: Missions' New Frontier* (Grand Rapids: Baker Book House, 2000), p. 55.

[3]Stewart Custer, *Witness to Christ* (Greenville, S.C.: BJU Press, 2000), p. 162.

[4]Greenway, p. 59.

[5]Logos Library System, *Advanced Strong's Concordance.*

[6]Greenway, p. 56.

[7]Dr. and Mrs. Howard Taylor, *J. Hudson Taylor* (Chicago: Moody Press, 1978), p. 217.

[8]Warren Wiersbe, *On Being a Servant* (Grand Rapids: Baker Book House, 1993), p. 4.

[9]Joseph H. Thayer, *Thayer's Greek-English Lexicon of the New Testament* (Grand Rapids: Baker Book House, 1981), p. 666.

[10]Rick Barry, "We'll Come Back for You," *Frontline Magazine* 10, no. 4 (July-August, 2000): p. 38.

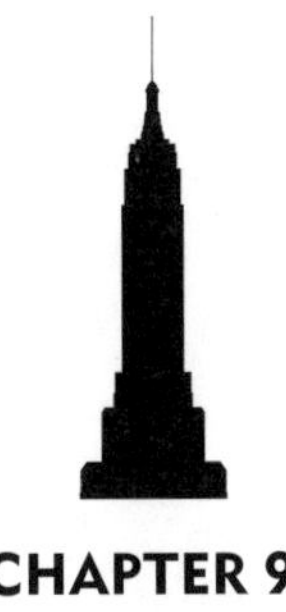

CHAPTER 9

THE CRY FROM THE CITY

One evening I entered a Brooklyn apartment near our church on Flatbush Avenue. The door to Randy's apartment was never locked so I pushed it open and entered. Darkness dominated this domain, except for a flicker of light at the end of the hall. The sticky wood floor was caked with dirt, and empty bottles littered the hallway. An old stove thrown into the bathroom sat awkwardly in the tub. As I entered the main room with a man from our church, forlorn men sat on broken-down chairs, mattresses, and couches. It looked like a human junkyard. I could see Slim sprawled on a couch, overcome with wine after a day of constant drinking. Slim was a drunkard who slurred and stuttered when he spoke. The alcohol had damaged his brain and ruined his life. There were others in the room, but I could not make out their faces. On the floor in the middle of this apartment sat an old paint tray. In the paint tray burned a single candle, the only light in the entire residence. That little candle flickered against the saddened faces of these men. It made them look like hulks of ruined humanity. It seemed they lived by a flicker of light with only a thread of hope. They were living in darkness as mere shadows of what God had created them to be, children of God for the praise of His glory. I shared with these men the love and light of the Lord Jesus Christ, but my words did not seem to penetrate the darkness of their hearts and minds. Soon after, Slim would enter a hospital, never to leave. He died and entered eternity. I can almost hear Slim cry in that stammering voice of his, "Come over and help us." Even that flickering flame shouts to me in silence, "Come over and help us," for souls are living in the darkness and face an eternity of destruction without Jesus Christ. This same cry from the man of Macedonia I call "the cry from the city," for it led Paul to the great cities of Macedonia.

As Paul ministered on his second missionary journey, he had trouble with direction. He sought to go into Asia, but the Holy Spirit forbade him (Acts 16:6). He tried to go into Bithynia, but "the Spirit suffered them not" (Acts 16:7). In the midst of his confusion the Lord sent a brief vision full of emotion to lead Paul into the major urban areas of his day. This vision would change the direction of Paul's life, for from that point forward, he would engage himself with the greatest cities of his world. "And a vision appeared to Paul in the night; There stood a man of Macedonia, and prayed him, saying, Come over into Macedonia, and help us" (Acts 16:9). This was a cry from the city and it led Paul to the city. Macedonia, a geographic region of northern Greece, was a great population center in Paul's day, filled with a mixture of people from all over the world. A key road called the Egnatian Way passed through Macedonia. People in their travels from Rome in the west and Asia in the east passed through Macedonia. The world lived in Macedonia. This Macedonian man's cry echoed in the heart of Paul, calling him to reach people of every ethnic group from all over the world. Paul immediately obeyed God and entered into Macedonia, but where did he go in this area of northern Greece? Paul went to "Philippi, which is the chief city of that part of Macedonia." His first convert to Christ was Lydia, a woman of Thyatira. Thyatira was a city of Asia, and although the Holy Ghost had "forbidden" Paul to enter Asia (Acts 16:6) earlier on this journey, the first soul "whose heart the Lord opened" (Acts 16:14) was a woman from Asia! God did not lead Paul to Asia at this point in his ministry because he could reach Asia in an ethnic center like Philippi. After Paul left Philippi, he went to the largest city of Macedonia, Thessalonica (Acts 17:1). The remainder of the Acts of the Apostles reveals the steps of Paul as he entered the main cities of his generation with the gospel of Christ: Berea, Athens, Corinth, Ephesus, Jerusalem, and finally Rome.

AN OPPORTUNITY TO REACH SOULS

We see in the Macedonian's cry, "Come over . . . and help us," the *opportunity* we have to go with the gospel. Urban ministry allows a greater than usual opening to reach souls from varied cultures for Christ. Everyone likes to "catch a break." In America we have caught a great spiritual break in that our population centers are filled with souls. Priceless people from all over the world now meet in our metropolitan areas. Many immigrants, some from countries traditionally "closed" to the gospel, flood into cities on a short-term basis to attend universities or to learn at a prestigious hospital. These newcomers are often the future leaders of their nations in politics, medicine, and business. Many other settlers from abroad come looking for the opportunities our free society affords.

The phrase "come over" conveys that we must pass over in spite of difficulties and obstructions. This exact construction "come over" in the original language appears in just two other places in our New Testament. In Hebrews 11:29 we see it in reference to Israel's crossing through the Red Sea on dry ground: "By faith they passed through the Red sea as by dry land: which the Egyptians assaying to do were drowned." The people of Israel by faith trusted the power of God to hold back the forces of the tides. Open doors do not necessarily mean easy opportunities; next door to the open door may be opposition. Paul decided at another point in his ministry to stay in the city of Ephesus in spite of opposition because he saw the opportunity: "For a great door and effectual is opened unto me, and there are many adversaries" (I Corinthians 16:9). Realizing that opposition and opportunity go together, we also must be willing to go, stand, and speak to reach those who cry, "Come over . . . and help us."

We also see this phrase "come over" in Luke 16:26. Abraham spoke as God's representative to the rich man in hell. The rich man begged for Lazarus to come with just a drop of water to cool his tongue. Abraham solemnly answered, "And beside all this, between us and you there is a great gulf fixed: so that they which would pass from hence to you cannot." Abraham declared the truth that once death opens its mouth and hell closes its door upon a lost soul, there is no hope or occasion for salvation. We cannot pray for loved ones who die; they are either in heaven or hell.

Scott and I went out on visitation. Scott was a vibrant young man who taught Sunday school at our fellowship. Around the corner from our church was a furniture store, and Alton worked there. He was poor, rail thin, and nearly toothless. His eyes looked at you with an empty stare that communicated a life vacant of hope. Scott and I approached Alton and asked him if we could share the gospel of salvation with him. Somewhat indifferently, Alton said no with a shake of his head. A few days later, Alton's brother told me Alton had been shot in the back on a block notorious for drugs. He lay in a hospital bed in critical condition. I went to the hospital to visit him, and he could not speak, but he could lightly squeeze my hand. I took Alton's hand, and for the second time I asked him if he would like for me to share the gospel of Christ's salvation with him. He gently squeezed my hand to signify that he would listen to how he could be saved. I explained the whole gospel to him and along the way asked him to squeeze my hand if he could understand. At each point I would feel a gentle squeeze. "Alton, do you realize you are a sinner? Do you understand that the wages of sin is death? Do you believe Christ died for your sins? Would you confess Him with your mouth and believe in Him from your heart?" Finally I prayed with him the sinner's prayer for salvation. I asked him, "Alton, did you just believe on Christ? Squeeze my hand if you did." I felt his hand weakly grip mine. Only God knows the decision of his heart, but I sensed that as long as he could breathe, the opportunity to help him existed. Not long after this, Alton died. We have an opportunity, but men are dying, and we must reach them with the gospel.

This cry from the city that led Paul to the city is a call that still remains. We must hear this cry and go to the city while we still have opportunity to preach the gospel of Christ's salvation. We must cross over in spite of obstacles, and we must pass over the same way Israel passed over the Red Sea: by faith!

The city of New York with its 308.9 square miles has nearly 24,000 people per square mile. One day I picked up an atlas and discovered that this great city has more people in it than forty-three of our fifty states. I continued analyzing and started adding up the populations of the least populated states in our nation. I added together ten states before I surpassed the population of New York City. Those states had an average density of seven people per square mile. I was challenged again with the great break we have caught to reach such a large number of people in a small area.

In the past fifty years New York City has changed. In 1950, New York City was 91 percent white and 9 percent black. In the most recent 2000 census, the Big Apple was 35 percent white, 25 percent black, 27 percent Hispanic, 10 percent Asian, and 4 percent multirace or other. This diversity will move eventually to the suburbs and villages of our nation. Are we ready to reach the uttermost part of the world when they come to our stable little towns? I fear that American Fundamentalism is unwilling to adapt to cultural change. I fear that we will fail to adjust to the changing ethnic classes and colors of people when they move out of the cities and into our suburbs. I have this fear because this has happened already in our American cities.

One reason American cities are such vast mission fields is that when foreign immigrants began moving into our cities after 1950, Christians ran away! Many churches, rather than adjust and reach the new wave of immigrants, moved away and basically abandoned ministry in those communities. Once-vibrant churches became empty shells. White flight within biblical Christianity is a sad historical fact we must face. In our new millennium, as the immigrants of all colors move out of our cities and into middle class suburbs, even rural areas will take on an urban flavor. American suburbs will change in color and culture in the next fifty years, and we must be ready to see the open door of opportunity. We must see this as a historic moment to reach the mission field in our own suburbs and cities. It is hypocritical of us to send missionaries to reach varied cultures in Africa, Asia, or some Hispanic nation and then refuse to reach them when they move next door. It is even more hypocritical to run away. As the color of America becomes more diverse, the color of American Fundamentalism must also change!

Perhaps Paul learned the blessing of cultural diversity in ministry from the church at Antioch, which commissioned him (Acts 13:1-3). The Antioch assembly demonstrated great unity with cultural diversity; this diversity existed within the congregation and also among the leadership of the church. Of the five prophets and teachers in the church, two were Jewish (Barnabas and Saul), two were from African nations (Niger and Lucius of Cyrene), and one was Roman, Manaen (Acts 13:1). Manaen was a childhood friend of Herod Antipas and had come from an elite social class.[1] How many churches today have such united acceptance of all ethnic cultures? Sad but true, some Bible-believing churches have retreated from the ethnic diversity inherent in cities and have moved to the suburbs, where there will not be any controversy over color. Those raised in socially elite classes do not want to count themselves with people from lower cultures. May God give us grace to attain ethnic diversity, not because society tells us we must have racial quotas but because we are training souls regardless of color or culture. The soul of man has no color. Paul's desire to reach any person of any color or class for Christ challenges us to do the same.

AN URGENCY TO REACH SOULS

The second aspect of this cry is the *urgency* of the man of Macedonia. The phrase "help us" comes from two words in the original language: "to shout" and "to run." The cry of this man was desperate and frantic. He was saying, "I am shouting to you in order that you will run and meet my need." If we are ever going to respond to the cry of the world, we must see the need as great. People in our cities are lonely, insecure, confused, cynical, and empty. Nevertheless, God works in hearts so that men and women cry out for help. Grief-stricken parents still cry out for their children under Satan's power: "If thou canst do any thing, have compassion on us, and *help* us" (Mark 9:22). Those who realize their blind condition still cry out, "Thou Son of David, have *mercy* on me" (Mark 10:48). The lost still cry, "What must I do to be *saved*." God still knows how to shake up a secure man's world and wake him up to his spiritual need. The Philippian jailer called for a light and then called upon the Light of the world. Where can people find help, mercy, and salvation but in our sinless Savior?

People will find what they really need in the gospel of the Lord Jesus Christ. Paul responded to this man's "911" cry for help by going into Macedonia. I marvel at Paul's instant response to charge into this ethnic melting pot. He saw the eternal gravity of the situation. "And after *he* had seen the vision, immediately *we* endeavoured to go into Macedonia, assuredly gathering that the Lord had called us for to preach the gospel unto them" (Acts 16:10). Paul did not delay helping those in Macedonia because he possessed what they needed. Luke joined Paul's missionary team at this point as the pronoun changes from "he" to "we." The writer, Luke, also became a part of Paul's crisis brigade. The greatest help that can be given to anyone is the preaching of the gospel; those without the gospel are in the greatest need of help. The good news of Jesus is what people need to hear to find real mercy and salvation: "Christ died for our sins according to the scriptures; and that he was buried, and that he rose again the third day according to the scriptures" (I Corinthians 15:3-4).

New York City has the best pizza in the world and I have eaten the best. I don't think I could make it a week without a good slice of New York City style pizza! When I eat pizza from a chain known for its delivery, I wonder how they survive. The cheese tastes cheap and the sauce salty. Then I realize that their success depends upon delivering the pizza fast and hot. Their motto is "We deliver." I see those pizza chains throughout New York City even though they compete against the best pizza in the world. They deliver more efficiently than anyone else; their techniques for timely delivery set the trend for everyone else. Not only do they survive; they thrive. Similarly, one does not have to be the best preacher to have a growing church that glorifies God in the city. One must deliver the good news of the righteousness of Jesus Christ to our world. We should have as our motto "We deliver the good news fast and hot!" Do you deliver the gospel with a heart set on fire by the Word of God and prayer?

I marvel at all the little storefronts in our city that paint fingernails and toenails. In the past ten years, they have sprung up everywhere. People have a vain concern about painting their toenails in our city! While our world worries about colorful toenails, we ought to be concerned about having beautiful feet "that bringeth good tidings, that publisheth peace; that bringeth good tidings of good, that publisheth salvation; that saith unto Zion, Thy God reigneth" (Isaiah 52:7). Paint on toenails wears off; preaching the gospel wins the lost to the righteous rule of Jesus Christ for all eternity. Do you have beautiful feet? Do you have a sense of urgency to preach Christ to the multitudes?

The social problems in our major cities appear humanly overwhelming. The problems of homelessness, homosexuality, poverty, drugs, divorce, domestic abuse, violent crime, and teenage pregnancy cause people to feel that we cannot help people with their real problems unless we provide them help with physical needs. This way of thinking is misguided. Biblical Fundamentalism has long rejected the social gospel, but it seems we have also turned our back on modern cities because of the immense social problems that plague them. When we look at the city, we wrongly conclude that we cannot succeed there. Roger Greenway in his book *Cities: Missions' New Frontier* says, "Americans hate failure and adore success. We tend to set goals for our lives and ministries that aren't easy to achieve in cities. This may explain why so many of the more gifted ministers and ambitious workers look elsewhere for their challenges. Our view of cities needs to be changed before this barrier disappears. At the same time our definitions of success, discipleship, and fruitful ministry need serious overhauling."[2]

We are not called to serve charitable causes at the expense of preaching and teaching the whole counsel of God. We can have a successful ministry in God's sight that wins the lost and disciples souls in the faith without having a homeless shelter or a food pantry. Let us never forget that to preach the gospel is to give man what he really needs. The gospel meets man in his greatest area of weakness: his lack of righteousness. Man cannot save himself and become right before God in his own strength, but the gospel is the power of God unto salvation. Man must meet the foe of death by standing in Christ's righteousness, for without Him none can conquer the last enemy of death. Jesus came to grant eternal life as a gift of His divine grace. The gospel fills full the deepest need man possesses. God gives a man doomed to die eternal life here and now! God translates the believing sinner "into the kingdom of His dear Son." God abundantly provided to save us from the power of darkness and eternal damnation; other issues pale in comparison to our predicament of facing a holy God. We should never delay running to help others in their need to find life, thinking that we don't have what they really need.

Nevertheless, let us not forget that preaching the whole counsel of God should also cause us to have a heart to meet the physical needs of those who lack. The hungry need food. The homeless need shelter.

The drug abuser needs a place to get off the street and away from temptation. As God provides the resources and the workers, we can initiate ministries that meet the physical needs of man. In going to urban areas, we may not be able to immediately establish such ministries, but we can go immediately and preach the gospel. As God gives us a foothold in the city, we can establish the other aspects of ministry to meet the needs of the physical man. The point is this: let us not reject the cities because of their social need merely because we have rejected the social gospel.[3] Yes, our cities need Christian schools, rescue missions, Christian colleges, and Christian drug and alcohol centers. Establishing such ministries requires a tremendous amount of resources. None of these can replace the preaching of the gospel and the importance of establishing local churches. Our lack of resources must not cause us to neglect our going into major urban areas, for we have the gospel of Jesus Christ, which can effect immediate change in any person who believes!

OVERCOMING DIFFICULTY TO REACH SOULS

As Paul answered this cry, it led him into the jaws of *difficulty*. Paul cast out a demon from a woman and ended up publicly beaten and bruised and cast into an inner prison, dark and damp. Along with Silas, Paul could have given an "organ recital" in solitary confinement. "Oh, my head, oh, my back, oh, my stomach," he could have moaned. Rather, Paul and Silas sang a dynamic duet and gave praise to God. Their shouts of joy brought down the house with a mighty earthquake! Paul had difficulty, but he gave God praise in the midst of the darkness.

People often ask me if I have had any dangers or difficulties in New York City. I must answer, "Compared to Paul, no!" I have had some minor incidents, however. On a beautiful sun-soaked Thursday that also happened to be July 4, I saw a young man wanted by the police for assaulting a police officer. I called the local precinct, and they chased the wanted felon up onto some nearby train tracks. Then they sent a police helicopter to look for the hiding outlaw. After the helicopter flew away, I heard an angry knock on our church door. It was the mother of the suspect. She angrily asked me one question: "Did you call the cops on my son?" I did not really want to tell the truth at that point, but neither did I desire to lie, so I stammered and stuttered. You see, this lady ran a drug-dealing business out of a candy store right next to our church. Her children even came to our Sunday school and Children's Week Day Bible Club activities. I spoke with the drug dealers regularly in this southeast section of Queens about Christ's salvation. One evening the dealers had even stashed their crack cocaine in our church mailbox. After the mother left, the police sent a special police unit in a van. They had shotguns and bulletproof vests. When I saw the police SWAT unit looking around the candy store next to our storefront church for the suspect, I thought it time to go home for the day. I walked across the street to my car while a group of fifteen to twenty drug dealers watched the police. Police presence always draws a crowd. The dealers started shouting to me, "Snitches get stitches," and other threats and curses. Two days later, on Saturday, I was inside the church with another man from our fellowship. We heard the sound of automatic gunfire outside the church. When we left the church after finishing our work, I went to my car. I began to drive away and discovered I had two flat tires. I got out of my car and saw the mother of the wanted man approaching me with what looked like the weapon we had heard while we were inside the church. Nearly at a loss for words, but not completely, at the top of my lungs I shouted, "Praise the Lord!" When in doubt, give thanks! I got back in my car and pulled a U-turn and drove away with two flat front tires on my front-wheel drive Honda Civic. Needless to say, my traction was not very good as I tried to maneuver my car away from potential danger. That day a group of teenage boys from Broomfield, Colorado, arrived to help with a week of vacation Bible school. They were scheduled to sleep in the church. When I told the pastor of the church about the incident, he decided that the Lord would protect them and that they would not run from their ministry or their sleeping quarters. I went to the police and reported the incident, and they provided us with a police officer each day on foot patrol. The Lord greatly blessed our week of ministry as we saw many children profess Jesus Christ as their personal Savior. As a matter of fact, two close relatives of the woman who came after me with the gun also came to our V.B.S. Their names were Theodore and Boom-Bay, and they even professed Jesus Christ as their Savior.

VICTORY IN REACHING SOULS

As Paul rejoiced in the midst of difficulty, God gave him a great *victory*. We would see more victories in our lives if we learned better to sing praises in the middle of dark times. God can save souls *under the power of darkness.* Sometimes the least likely people in the least likely places are saved! The cold-hearted "correctional officer" did not seem impressed with Paul's singing in solitary confinement since he fell into a deep sleep. Violent and brutal, this jailer appeared reckless and indifferent about God, eternity, and the souls of men. He demonstrated violence when he coldly "thrust" Paul into that inner prison. What we outwardly see is not always the whole story.

God has a way of suddenly getting a hardheaded man's attention! The jailer saw the hand of God in the sudden earthquake. Jarred from his deep sleep, he rightly feared death when he supposed the prisoners under his authority had fled. Standing *on* the very *doorstep of death* and just a heartbeat from hell, the jailer took a sword to plunge into his chest. He could find no point in living another moment until Paul bravely stood between him and eternal judgment.

Many commit suicide when they "suppose" incorrectly. Reasoning with someone who has no hope is difficult. When individuals suppose their depression has no end, when they suppose their problems have no answer (King Saul), when they suppose their loss is life shattering (Zimri, I Kings 16:18), when they suppose no one loves them or ever will, when they suppose they are a failure (Ahithophel,

II Samuel 17:23), or when they suppose they will never change (Judas, Matthew 27:5), suicide is often the next step.

Suicide is the deliberate taking of one's life; it is a permanent solution to a temporary problem. It is the ultimate cry for help, but it is a final cry, for the suicide victim goes beyond help. Suicide is an extreme form of selfish communication and self-love. For some, like this jailer, suicide may be considered a foolish act of bravery to communicate their fearlessness toward death. An estimated twenty-six thousand Americans annually commit suicide. Teenagers especially commit suicide at alarming rates: they seek to gain attention, punish surviving family members or friends, or think they will join a friend who has died. It is the number two killer among teens; it is estimated that six thousand teens kill themselves each year in the United States. One suicide every fifteen minutes is attempted. One every thirty minutes succeeds. Twenty-five percent of females who attempt suicide were sexually abused. Three times as many men kill themselves as women, yet three times as many women attempt suicide. Some warning signs typical in suicide victims are verbal threats, preoccupation with themes of death, dramatic and sudden problems in home and school, abuse of drugs and alcohol, and chronic guilt.[4]

Paul showed wisdom in counseling this jailer on the brink of death. He gave him hope by telling him the facts: "Do thyself no harm: for we are all here" (Acts 16:28). Most people who attempt suicide want to be stopped and can be stopped if someone will lovingly talk to them and stand in their way. People do not really want to end their life; they want to end their pain. Paul openly and biblically confronted this man with his behavior and took his actions very seriously.

This jailer moved from the power of darkness and doorstep of death *into the family of God.* God's powerful shaking of the earth led this trembling jailer to cry out, "What must I do to be saved?" Miraculously, he followed Paul's command to believe on the Lord Jesus Christ. God convicted his heart at his place of employment; then Paul went to his home and proclaimed Christ to his whole family.

Maybe you work in a prison or a police precinct. Perhaps you work in an office or a public school. There are people around you with real problems. You do not have to wait for them to enter the church doors to tell them of Christ. Walking down an aisle in a church service is not the only time people may come to Christ. This jailer was saved amidst the rubble of the dungeon at midnight; his family came to Christ in their home. The best time to talk to someone about salvation may be at a coffee break at work or at the kitchen table of their own home. Personally, I have seen more lasting salvation professions in the convert's home than anywhere else. I am able to listen better, as well as allow the one to whom I am talking to share his spiritual relationship more thoroughly, so that I can speak to his need wisely.

Edna attended our church one day, listened to the service, and went home without speaking to anyone. She did leave her visitor card in the offering plate, so I called her on the phone. Edna, a seventy-three-year-old woman who had attended the Episcopal Church her whole life, was not sure of her salvation. I sat at her kitchen table and asked some simple questions about her spiritual life. We were both relaxed and not in a hurry, which sometimes is not the case during a church invitation or after a church service. I was able to listen to her and find out her spiritual condition. I discovered she had never been born again, so I gave her the good news that she could believe in Jesus Christ and have His righteousness imputed to her. Edna repented and became a baptized member of our church. It seemed so easy, for God evidently was drawing her to Himself.

This believing jailer evidenced an immediate and remarkable change in character. Deliverance from the power of darkness and entrance into the family of God leads to a radical transformation. What an example of repentance is this jailer! One moment he behaved in a heartless manner, shutting Paul in the inner prison. As a child of God, he brought the man of God into his own home to clean out Paul's wounds and feed him a decent meal. His violence was transformed into mercy. Moments earlier he feared the prisoners had fled and he nearly committed suicide. As a child of God he allowed Paul and Silas to leave the prison so that he and his whole family could follow the Lord in believer's baptism and rejoice with them over their new life in Christ! His selfishness was transformed into hospitality. He was baptized and his hopelessness was transformed into joy. Seeing people trust Christ and then evidence Christ's life is an incomparable joy. On the other hand, seeing people "accept Christ" and then never show any evidence of life or salvation is a great frustration. We must carefully counsel the lost so that we do not force them into decisions if there is no conviction of sin or real faith in Christ. In urban areas we can see many "decisions" that never result in "conversion."

One evening, a lady named Louisa, from Grenada, came into our services. She filled out the visitor card and also filled out three words on her card as a prayer request. Louisa wrote that she desired "to find Jesus." I translate those three words "Come over and help us!" I called and discovered she had listened to Christian radio for over ten years, but she was still living in doubt concerning her salvation. It was not a difficult task to show Louisa I John 5:10-13 and encourage her to take God at His Word. "He that hath the Son hath life; and he that hath not the Son of God hath not life," the Scripture says. She rested in the promise of God and became a Lydia to us in our church as one of our most faithful members.

Many today cry out like the man of Macedonia; souls live in the darkness of sin on the doorstep of death. Ask God to give you a tender heart to hear the cries of those around you so that you obey the heavenly vision and endeavor to share the gospel with those in need. You can reach people of any culture by the power of God. You can hear those cries when you *see* souls living in darkness with only a thread of hope. You can hear those cries when you *feel* the gentle squeeze of a dying man upon your hand. You can hear those cries when you *read* that someone needs Jesus. Men and women still cry from the city: "Come over . . . and help us!"

---

[1]Stewart Custer, *Witness to Christ* (Greenville, S.C.: BJU Press, 2000), p. 182.

[2]Roger S. Greenway and Timothy M. Monsma, *Cities: Missions' New Frontier* (Grand Rapids: Baker Book House, 2000), p. 94.

[3]Greenway, p. 95.

[4]Freedom Flyer Ministries Criminal Justice Chaplaincy Training Manual, Book Two.

CHAPTER 10

The Focus That Conquers Fear in the City

Sometimes people ask why I am in New York City. I never received a vision, had a dream, or saw a message written in the sky. After my conversion, I simply saw and experienced the need in New York City. I saw for myself multitudes who lived without the Shepherd for their soul.

I was raised in Cresskill, New Jersey, a suburb just fifteen minutes northwest of the George Washington Bridge. The Lord led me to attend a good Bible-believing church in Manhattan in the summer of 1978. I had just been saved in April of that year during my freshman year at Clemson University in South Carolina. Our Manhattan church had a visitation program and I began to go out on the streets with others in the church to witness. The need of lost people trapped in sin, drugs, alcohol, and fornication occupied my thoughts as I considered my future.

As I read the Bible, certain verses on the city were deeply impressed upon my heart. The word "city" began to jump out at me and I began to behold the city from a biblical perspective. I began to see the city throughout Scripture. No other verse in the Bible has so gripped me for the great work of urban ministry than Acts 18:10: "For I am with thee, and no man shall set on thee to hurt thee: for I have much people in this city." I will never forget praying over this verse on a rainy day, in the front seat of my Chevrolet Nova, while I was a graduate student at Bob Jones University in Greenville, South Carolina. God used this verse to indelibly burden me for the city. He also used this verse to comfort me regarding my fears of urban ministry. Would I be safe? Would I fail? Would God provide? God calmed my spirit with His promise. Perhaps the Lord can use this verse to give you the right focus to conquer any fear in your heart related to ministry in a metropolitan area.

THE GRASSHOPPER MENTALITY

A large city has a way of making a man feel very small. This sense of smallness leads naturally to fear. When the twelve spies searched the land of Canaan, do you remember their assessment? "The land whither thou sentest us . . . floweth with milk and honey . . . nevertheless the people be strong that dwell in the land, and the cities are walled, and very great: and moreover we saw the children of Anak there" (Numbers 13:27-28). The land was great but the people and the walls intimidated the people of God. There were giants! As the Israelites appraised themselves, they concluded, "we were in our own sight as grasshoppers, and so we were in their sight" (Numbers 13:33). Here lies a key reason many Christians avoid the city for ministry: the "grasshopper mentality." We come to a wrong perspective of the situation because we focus on the wrong things. We also feel small and become afraid when we look at the walls of difficulty, the giants of opposition, and our own human weakness. Caleb and Joshua maintained the right focus even though they saw the same giants and the same walls as the other spies. They focused upon the land and the Lord. "The land, which we passed through to search it, is an exceeding good land. If the Lord delight in us, then he will bring us into this land, and give it us; a land which floweth with milk and honey" (Numbers 14:7-8).

When I first went into New York City, I said, "How can I ever reach this place?" It seemed so big, and I was so small. New York City still seems immense, and I often feel insignificant, but I know how we can reach it: one soul at a time. New York City is a spiritual battleground the fearful fail to enter; New York City is a battleground for the fearless. How can we overcome fear to fulfill God's call to the city? What focus can conquer our fears? When the grasshopper mentality invades my soul, I remember that in God's sight I am not a grasshopper, for He has called me an ambassador, a king, and a priest for Jesus Christ (Revelation 1:6).

In Acts 18, the apostle Paul entered into the mighty city of Corinth. Immorality and drunkenness prevailed in this ancient metropolis. "To Corinthianize" meant to engage in prostitution; Corinth flourished as the Gomorrah of Paul's day. While he ministered in Corinth, he wrote the Epistle to the Romans and expounded in detail the depravity of pagan man (Romans 1:18-32). This pagan behavior Paul described in Romans 1 brazenly displayed itself in the Corinthian culture. Corinth reigned as the political center of Greece; accordingly, it was the center of commerce between Europe and Asia. In this growing city lived all nations of people who came to Corinth in order to partake of the financial opportunities that abounded. Through the streets of Corinth thronged travelers and traders from every country known to man. In the daytime the markets swarmed with soldiers, sailors, slaves, athletes, betting men, and religious people. In the night its streets rang out with the songs of drunken revelry and the sounds of moral sins.

While he was in Corinth, fear struck deeply into Paul's heart and tempted him to remain silent. Paul experienced this trepidation in spite of having close friendships with Aquila and Priscilla, Titus, and Timothy (Acts 18:1-5). Dread gripped Paul even though he had boldly reasoned in the synagogue and fully absorbed himself with the preaching of the gospel. Paul's fear actually came from an unexpected source; he was having success in reaching souls for Christ. "Crispus, the chief ruler of the synagogue, believed on the Lord with all his house; and many of the Corinthians hearing believed, and were baptized" (Acts 18:8). Paul feared these conversions would bring about hostility from the Jews. He had already faced great opposition after successes in Philippi and Thessalonica; now he feared more of the same. Fear is a normal part of urban ministry. Paul entered Corinth "in weakness, and in fear, and in much trembling" (I Corinthians 2:3). The best of men fight fear. Paul was afraid even to the point of silence! The best of believers have times of brightness and times of darkness; the best of believers have times of shining for Christ and times of exhaustion. God knew Paul's heart, and the Lord spoke a word of comfort: "Be not afraid, but speak, and hold not thy peace" (Acts 18:9). What a promise Paul received! God told Paul, "Do not be afraid; focus upon Me."

FOCUS ON GOD'S PRESENCE

Christians first must focus upon God's *presence.* "For I am with thee" (Acts 18:10*a*). In a great big place with great walls and great giants, it is easy to feel intimidated. The first time I drove through Flatbush, Brooklyn, my heart panicked as I looked upon all the unfamiliar faces, the different cultures, the litter, the graffiti, and the cars speeding through the streets. In places that alarm us we must remember the promise of the presence of God. "Lo, I am with you alway, even unto the end of the world" (Matthew 28:20*b*). In the Scripture, the presence of God calms the violent storms, opens raging rivers, quenches mighty fires, shuts the mouths of lions, and gives direction when we do not know what to do. His presence gives peace when everything falls apart around us, for He says, "I am with you."

One of God's favorite commands is "Fear not!" It seems God says this about three hundred sixty-five and one quarter times in the Bible: one for every day of the year! God spoke these words to Abraham when doubt began to overcome him (Genesis 15:1). God said "fear not" to Isaac when the enemies kept stealing his wells

(Genesis 26:24). God said "fear not" to Jacob when he was about to go to Egypt to reunite with Joseph (Genesis 46:3). God said "be not afraid" to Joshua as he took over the leadership of Israel to lead them over into the land of promise: "Be not afraid, neither be thou dismayed: for the Lord thy God is with thee whithersoever thou goest" (Joshua 1:9). God said "fear not" to Israel many times as they prepared to return out of Babylonian captivity: "Fear thou not; for I am with thee: be not dismayed; for I am thy God: I will strengthen thee; yea, I will help thee; yea, I will uphold thee with the right hand of my righteousness" (Isaiah 41:10; see also Isaiah 43:1-5; Isaiah 44:2-8). The Lord Jesus told Peter to "fear not" when He called him to stop catching fish to fish for men (Luke 5:10). The angel of God told Paul to "fear not" as he sailed for Rome during the dark, hurricane-like winds when everyone else had lost all hope of survival (Acts 27:24). God has promised, "I will never leave thee, nor forsake thee. So that we may boldly say, The Lord is my helper, and I will not fear what man shall do unto me" (Hebrews 13:5*b*-6). We have no reason to fear because we are not alone. God is with us! General Patton, the World War II hero, said, "All men are afraid in the battle, the coward is the one who lets his fear overcome his sense of duty."

FOCUS ON GOD'S PROTECTION

The second vital focus we need in order to conquer fear is to rely on God's *protection.* God assured Paul, "no man shall set on thee to hurt thee" (Acts 18:10*b*). The hour of success had brought opposition to Paul in Philippi and Thessalonica. He now feared further trouble after the salvation of Crispus and many of the Corinthians. God's Word was tested and found true. The Jews rose up against Paul and brought him before Gallio, the political deputy of Achaia. No doubt this Jewish delegation led by Sosthenes wanted Paul beaten and jailed. They cried, "This fellow persuadeth men to worship God contrary to the law" (Acts 18:13), but the deputy decided not to do anything to Paul. "He drave them from the judgment seat" (Acts

18:16). Gallio did not want to get into the middle of their religious disputes, so he rid himself of their quarrel. However, the townspeople did not display such nonchalance toward this dispute. They actually turned in anger against the leader of the Jews, Sosthenes, and had him battered instead of Paul! This is probably the same Sosthenes who later was saved and joined Paul in writing to the same Corinthians a few years later (I Corinthians 1:1). This beating turned into a great blessing for Sosthenes, for he saw the power of God's promise to protect Paul. In the midst of all this, Gallio remained defiantly inattentive to the conflict occurring in his own courtroom. As Sosthenes was beaten before the judgment seat, Gallio "cared for none of those things" (Acts 18:17).

God has mercifully protected our family in the city. One morning after our nursing home ministry, Debbie thought she would take our two small children in their double stroller for a walk around the block before returning to our apartment to make lunch. As she pushed the stroller, she sang the little chorus "If the Lord is in your heart today, and He's taken all your sins away." She could sense someone coming up behind her, and she also felt like she should keep singing that song. Debbie continued: "You can walk each mile with a happy smile." She turned around to see who was coming up behind her. It was a young man with a dagger in his hand. He was holding it up to his neck. Debbie turned around and finished the song: "If the Lord is in your heart today."

The young man pulled up evenly with Debbie and said, "Do you have any money?"

Debbie showed him her empty pockets. Then she said, "No, but this reminds me of when someone asked Peter and John for money and they said, 'Silver and gold have I none; but such as I have give I thee: in the name of Jesus Christ of Nazareth rise up and walk.' Jesus has power and He saved me from my sins. Has anyone ever shared with you how you can be saved from your sins?"

The young man mumbled, "No." Debbie began sharing her testimony with the young man, and as she talked, the stalker put his knife away. They got to the end of the block and Debbie asked him which way he was going, for she had not finished sharing with him God's salvation! He again muttered, "Straight." Debbie went one more block with him and then returned home safely.

FOCUS ON GOD'S PEOPLE

We must also focus upon God's *people*. "I have much people in this city." The two little words "much people" are the burning words of this chapter. Yes, the fruit of ministry in the city is good, just as it was in the land of promise. There is fruit to harvest from all over the world. We should hunger to preach the gospel to people from all over the world, but alas, like the ten spies in the land of promise, we want to run in fear. Our focus is in the wrong place! Focus on the people. God is sovereign, and He is "not willing that any should perish," and He has "much people in this city!"

These two little words ought to *motivate us to be persistent*. People all around us search and hunger for the truth as God draws and convicts people of sin. God had jewels in the cesspool of iniquity in Corinth. I looked up the word "much" and discovered that "much" means "much"! "Much" does not mean that all will be saved. "Much" does not mean that none will be saved. "Much" simply means much. That God has "much people" gives us a responsibility to reach them, for "how then shall they call on him in whom they have not believed? and how shall they believe in him of whom they have not heard? and how shall they hear without a preacher?" (Romans 10:14). This verse gives us three questions with one answer: they will not! People will not call, believe, or hear of our Lord Jesus Christ without a preacher. God has ordained the preaching of the word "to save them that believe" (I Corinthians 1:21). Preaching the Word of God will never become outdated or obsolete, for God has sovereignly ordained this method until the end of the age. We must not apply the "what works mentality" to ministry. If some churches remove their pulpits and minimize preaching in favor of entertaining music or skits, we must reject such methodology. We are compelled to follow the Word of God, for preaching the Word (II Timothy 4:2) is God's unchanging, divine method to bring the truth to the lost. Paul "continued" or as the footnote in my Bible says, "sat there," among them for a year and a half because he believed what God said. We need the courage to sit and stay doing God's will! Our job is to acknowledge Him in faithfulness and obedience; God's work is to bring forth the fruit through our labor that "should remain" (John 15:16). God had "much people" and this motivated Paul to persist and to "endure all things for the elect's sakes, that they may also obtain the salvation which is in Christ Jesus with eternal glory" (II Timothy 2:10). The fact that God had these people did not cause Paul to be indolent but it motivated Paul to be persistent.

These two simple words also *guarantee to us fruit*. This promise not only demonstrates God's sovereignty in salvation but also confirms our responsibility to fearlessly function in the place where God has put us. He has "much people"; He elected them from the foundation of the world. Just as God said to Elijah that He had "seven thousand men, who have not bowed the knee to the image of Baal. Even so then at this present time also there is a remnant according to the election of grace" (Romans 11:4-5). This phrase challenges me greatly to go: "a remnant according to the election of grace"! Elijah ministered in a day when idolatry and Baal worship gripped the hearts of men. Neither Elijah nor Paul knew who these elect were or what their addresses or phone numbers were. The Word of God did guarantee them that they were there. Divine sovereignty and human responsibility do not collide, but they complement one another. C. H. Spurgeon said, "I never try to reconcile friends."

Now you say, "But how do we know who are elect?" We don't know! D. L. Moody said, "You have no more to do with the doctrine of election than you have with the government of China!" Since we do not know where the elect are, or who the elect are, we have to beat the bushes, pass out tracts, go door to door, witness on the subways and at bus stops and wherever God gives the opportunity. This promise of much people emphasizes our responsibility to sit down, to stay, and not to quit in our desire to win and disciple souls for the Lord Jesus Christ!

To produce fruit takes work. Ask any farmer! Just as a farmer must plow, plant, water, and care for the seed, so we must be willing to work in order to win souls and see "much people" come to Christ. One summer our church organized the distribution of over thirty thousand gospel tracts. We passed out different kinds of literature, from four-color church brochures to simple black-and-white gospel presentations. We shared these tracts in parks, on street corners, in subways, and under the doors of many apartment buildings. Out of that, three people visited our Sunday morning services and so far two of them continue to come! Realizing the value of one soul, how can one say that planting those seeds was not worth it? How do we know how God will use the seed planted in the days ahead? Perhaps someone will be saved next month or next year and start attending our church. Maybe they will go to another church, and we will never know until we get to heaven how our work resulted in the increase of God's kingdom. Perhaps one of those tracts will go to China or Africa and lead to the salvation of souls in another land. When one gives out a tract anywhere, but especially in an international city like New York, he never knows how far that tract will go. It may go to the uttermost, and it may also go into the "guttermost," that is, the nearest dumpster!

Finally, the promise of reaching God's people *demonstrates to us grace.* The city is full of people dying and people living, people young and people old. Where sin and corruption abound, so does heartache and heartbreak. Where there is anguish, there exist soul restlessness and searching. Where there is searching, the Holy Spirit is convicting souls over their sin and giving people an eagerness for and openness to the gospel. "But where sin abounded, grace did much more abound" (Romans 5:20*b*). God had "much people" in Nineveh during the days of Jonah, God had "much people" in Samaria while Philip ministered in that city (Acts 8:8), and I am convinced He has "much people" in our major cities today. We must be willing to go, overcome our fear, and continue in the city to reach the people.

OUT FROM THE WRONG CHURCH

Ina called on the phone one day after receiving at her door a gospel tract from our church. She asked for more detailed information about our ministry and promised she would come to church the next Sunday. Before the service that week, I saw a lady drive up to the church, and seeing she looked a little lost, I went over to her while she was still in the car. It was Ina. I greeted her and told her the service was about to begin and that I would meet her in the auditorium. I went into the church, and we began the service, but Ina never came in. I was afraid I had offended her in some way, so I went to her home the very next night. She gladly welcomed me into her kitchen, and I asked her, "Where did you go?" She looked at me and likewise said, "Where did *you* go?" Then it dawned upon me. She had gone into the wrong church! You see, there was another storefront church right beside ours, and she went into that service and had no desire to return to the church she had mistakenly attended. She did come to our church the next week and that Sunday she genuinely received the Lord Jesus Christ as her Savior. She grew in the grace of the Lord, was baptized, and invited many other people to our church as the living water of God's Holy Spirit flowed from her heart. Ina, whose spiritual gift was giving, would give to everyone she knew. One Sunday she saw that my watch was broken as I borrowed someone's watch in our choir during my morning sermon. I did not want to preach too long. After service that Sunday afternoon, my doorbell rang. Ina stood on my front porch and presented me with a brand-new Seiko watch!

A DEATH WARRANT ON HIS SOUL

A man named Joe heard me speak on the radio and called our church. Neither Joe nor I are mystics, but he had had a dream that he should attend a church in Manhattan in which the pastor's name was Matthew. Not long after that, he heard of our church through our Heritage of Faith radio program. Since my name is Matthew and we were in Manhattan, he called and I set an appointment to meet him. As we sat in a diner drinking coffee, I could see that the Lord had prepared him to hear and believe the gospel. Joe had left the Roman Catholic Church as a young teenager. His uncle, a Seventh-day Adventist, influenced him during his mid-teen years, but Joe had fallen away from attending any church.

As we sat and talked, I sensed the conviction of the Holy Spirit upon his heart. I asked him, "Joe, have you come to the place in your spiritual life that if you were to die tonight you know for sure that you would go to heaven?" He honestly answered, "No, that is what I am not sure about." I said, "Why don't we leave this restaurant and go to an area where we can privately talk." We walked over to the Hudson River and sat on a bench on a pier jutting out into the Hudson in the south part of Manhattan Island. I opened up a gospel tract called "The Bridge" and began giving him the gospel on that pier. I was going through the "Romans Road" when a bicycle accident happened ten yards from where we were sitting. What an interruption! We had looked at Romans 3:23 and Romans 6:23 and had just turned to Romans 5:8. A drunken man crashed headfirst into the concrete; he lay in a lump with his head gashed and bleeding. His brain was literally exposed. His shoulder was dislocated. Some bystanders called 911. I knelt down and asked his hysterical girlfriend if I could pray for them. The man with his head bleeding was nevertheless conscious and cursing up a storm. When I asked if I could pray, the girlfriend coldly and curtly told me, "Oh, shut up." I departed from them and prayed for them with Joe and another bystander. As I prayed, the sirens of the ambulance could be heard. As the ambulance technicians worked to bring the injured man to the hospital, I said to Joe, "What we are trying to do is even more important than what the EMS is trying to do. The ambulance team is seeking to see physical life saved; I am seeking to see you saved spiritually for all eternity." We sat down on the park bench and I continued giving him the gospel. Joe prayed with tears to believe on the Lord Jesus!

Joe later wrote to me about where he was that night I met him: "I was buried deep in sin before coming to Christ. I was a liar, and a cheat. I experimented with illegal drugs and alcohol and broke nearly every commandment of the Bible. I felt lost and without hope. I felt an emptiness that I could not describe and I still cannot. I felt the conviction of the Holy Spirit, and I knew then that I had a death warrant upon my life and I was headed straight to hell!"

Joe expressed his new life in the following way: "When I confessed my sins to my Father, and accepted the Lord Jesus Christ, I cried like I never had before. Jesus set me free from my sins and took the sadness out of my heart and filled it with joy. I was filled that night with the Holy Spirit and since that night I have experienced a growing fellowship with the Lord. I began to attend Heritage Baptist Church and was warmly welcomed as part of the family."

The biker survived that incident with a separated shoulder and a cracked head, and he had no brain damage, from what I understand. As far as I know, however, he has that "death warrant" on him. Joe was in church the Sunday after this incident, and he continues to give all the evidences of true conversion: repentance from his sin, faith in the crucified and risen Christ, and a new joy on the basis of the gift of God. Yes, God has "much people in this city."

Let us not allow fear to overcome our sense of duty. As we focus on God's presence, God's promise, and God's people, even we grasshoppers can overcome the fear that is natural in our human condition.

CHAPTER 11

How God Can Use Ordinary You . . . in the City

Our world has gone urban. In 1800, not one city in the Western world had over a million people. Only 3 percent of the world's population lived in a city larger than five thousand.[1] By 1900, 14 percent lived in urban areas and this number had jumped to 40 percent in 1980. By 2050, approximately 79 percent of the world's population will live in urban centers, with much of the growth coming from the urban explosion in Africa, Latin America, and Asia.[2] Nearly half of the urban population in the Southern Hemisphere live in squalid conditions or shantytowns. At the start of 1900 only twenty cities in the world exceeded one million inhabitants. Presently there are over two hundred thirty-five.[3]

In America, between 1790 and 1890, the total population grew 16-fold, but the urban population grew 139-fold. By 1920, the urban population exceeded 50 percent of the population with immigrants flooding in from Europe.[4] By 1950, almost 64 percent of North America's population was urban.[5] Numerical growth of cities in the Western world has leveled off because of a lack of space, but there is increasing internationalization of cities in the United States and Western Europe. If we are going to reach our world, we must reach our cities, not only in America, but worldwide. I believe God can use ordinary you in the city for His glory.

As Paul entered Ephesus, the temple of Diana sent dark shadows of superstition out of Ephesus into all of Asia and the whole known world. Ephesus, the most influential city in Asia Minor, also had a well-known theatre and seaport, but the temple was known best of all. This huge temple, one of the seven wonders of the world, set Ephesus apart as a city of renown. The temple to Diana was 425 feet long and 220 wide. Its 127 columns rose 60 feet into the air. This impressive structure brought spiritual destruction to all who worshiped the false goddess Diana. The idolatry of Diana led to immorality and every form of moral and spiritual uncleanness. Dens of prostitution were scattered all around Ephesus, and the earnings of the prostitute priestesses were given to the temple for the support and upkeep of this immoral idolatry. This humanly elegant edifice was empty of life-giving instruction; it was large, but helpless to grant salvation. How cold and dead was that temple! Nevertheless, to this stronghold of idolatry Paul carried the life-changing news of Jesus.

While Paul worked in Ephesus, God used him in an extraordinary ministry full of miracles. We today will not see the specific "signs and wonders" phenomenon that God did through Paul in the city of Ephesus.[6] For example, our new converts will not speak in tongues and prophesy (Acts 19:6). The gift of tongues was the miraculous ability to speak languages one had never studied. This supernatural gift was given for the purpose of presenting a sign to the nation of Israel of judgment to come (I Corinthians 14:21-22; Deuteronomy 28:46-51). It is my conviction that tongues ceased once Jerusalem was destroyed in A.D 70. Once the event to which a sign points does occur, the sign is unnecessary. In this case, the gift of tongues pointed to the judgment of Jerusalem; once this took place, the sign ceased.

God wrought other miracles through Paul in Ephesus that we do not expect to see in modern-day ministry. Our sweat will not bring about healing (Acts 19:12). Demons will not call out our name (Acts 19:15).

Our churches may never cause an economic firestorm (Acts 19:34). This does not mean God cannot or is not using us.

Urban ministries today emphasizing the importance of "signs and wonders" as an evidence of God's power still attract large numbers and fill large arenas. This delusion saddens me because the common urbanite is swept away by the emotional experience. Well-known Charismatic leaders teach that "God must be invited to 'confirm the word with signs following.'"[7] This is a dangerous interpretation of Hebrews 2:4. To such Charismatic leaders, rejecting signs, wonders, and extra-biblical revelation in this dispensation results in a barrenness of God's power. Those who hold to Pentecostal, experience-based theology accuse us who reject signs and wonders for today of accepting just a part of the promises of the Bible.[8] Jim Cymbala, well-known pastor of the Brooklyn Tabernacle, attacks non-Pentecostal churches as having "short-change[d] the gospel of Christ and the Holy Spirit." He writes that non-Charismatic churches have "institutionalized backsliddenness."[9] He writes concerning those of us who believe that the apostolic gift of signs and wonders was only for the apostles, "What a pathetic cop-out. What a rejection of the very Bible they boast in."[10] His attack is both unbiblical and unfortunate. I answer that it is not a matter of rejecting the Bible, but it is a matter of being satisfied with the Bible. We do not need "fresh revelation" in order to have "fresh power," "fresh wind," or "fresh fire." "An evil and adulterous generation seeketh after a sign," Jesus said (Matthew 12:39). If God wills not to miraculously shake the ground after I pray (Acts 4:31), send a miraculous sight of tongues sitting upon my head when I preach, send forth a miraculous sound of wind when I worship (Acts 2:2-3), or give a miraculous speech when I talk, I still believe all of the Bible. I still believe in the power of the Holy Spirit, the power of Christ's blood, the power of prayer, the power of Jesus' name, and the power of God's Word!

God did signs and wonders in the past to confirm His word according to His will. Fred Moritz has well written that Hebrews 2:1-4 "teaches that both the revelation and the accrediting signs and wonders have ceased."[11] Moritz correctly states that "Christ and the apostles were the ones chosen by God to give this revelation to men" and that "this passage 'slams the door' on any idea of a valid, biblically justified revelation from God in this age."[12]

I love Acts 19:11: "And God wrought special miracles by the hands of Paul." The miracles occurring in Ephesus were wrought by God through the hands of the apostle Paul. Being an apostle and an inspired author of nearly half the New Testament, Paul and his ministry were confirmed by God's signs and wonders. God did "signs and wonders, and with divers miracles, and gifts of the Holy Ghost, according to His own will" (Hebrews 2:4). The special miracles that God wrought through Paul in Ephesus were not duplicated in any other city where Paul preached. Paul never made tongues speaking a requirement for the "baptism of the Holy Spirit" in any city he entered on account of the miracle of tongues speaking in Ephesus. He did not start mailing out his sweaty shirts in every other city he entered after seeing God do that particular miracle in Ephesus. Paul accepted these miracles from God and never stereotyped these miraculous signs as the only evidences of God's power for a successful ministry. These miracles are not about *what Paul did,* but what God did through Paul.

We do not have to see extraordinary miracles to see God do great things. We do not have to be extraordinary apostles in order for God to use us. God can use ordinary you, even in a great modern-day city.

ORDINARY YOU CAN PERSONALLY MINISTER TO HUNGRY SOULS

In Acts 19:1, Paul found certain disciples of John the Baptist. Paul was aggressive in ministry and took the initiative, but it was God doing the work through him. "Whereunto I also labour, striving according to his working, which worketh in me mightily" (Colossians 1:29). Paul toiled tirelessly, but he knew consciously that God worked in him to work through him. God can use us to find disciples who need biblical direction for their lives.

In all three of the churches that we started, God led us to people who were already saved and looking for church fellowship. I gave a gospel tract to Rodney and his mother, Alexandrina, on the streets of Flatbush, Brooklyn. Saved in Grenada, West Indies, Rodney and "Sister Mac" needed a church to attend in their community. They came to the second Sunday service we had at City View Baptist Church, and they never stopped coming. The only regret I ever heard them express about our church is that they did not come to the first service! In Queens, while founding Parkway Baptist Church, I gave a church brochure to Evelyn. A believer from Jamaica, Evelyn needed to find a church like ours in her Queens neighborhood. I baptized Evelyn at a beach in Far Rockaway, and she continued faithfully in our fellowship. Whenever we needed a special song, she was ready! In Manhattan, Consuelo, a dear elderly woman from Spain, prayed for ten years for a church in her Chelsea area. We were the answer to her prayers when we started Heritage Baptist Church. Randy called me on the phone after hearing our radio broadcast. He, too, looked for a non-Charismatic church, and he brought a friend named Carmine. They both now serve as deacons in our Manhattan ministry. All along the way God has led us to disciples who need teaching and fellowship and who hunger to serve in a local church.

Next, Paul talked to those disciples and personally ministered to them. He discovered their spiritual condition by asking two penetrating questions that cut through their confusion: "Have ye received the Holy Ghost since ye believed? And they said unto him, We have not so much as heard whether there be any Holy Ghost. And he said unto them, Unto what then were ye baptized? And they said, Unto John's baptism" (Acts 19:2-3). We too can discover much about people's spiritual condition by asking them about their relationship to the Holy Spirit and their experience of water baptism. Paul realized that they were sincere but had not been fully taught. They had been baptized but had not heard about the powerful pouring out of the Holy Spirit on the Day of Pentecost. They were not baptized personally by John the Baptist but by a "well-meaning disciple of his, that ignorantly kept up his name as the head of a party, retaining the spirit and notion of those disciples of his that were jealous of the growth of Christ's interests."[13]

In Acts 19:4 Paul clarified the purpose of John's baptism. "Then said Paul, John verily baptized with the baptism of repentance, saying unto the people, that they should believe on him which should come after him, that is, on Christ Jesus." Paul made clear that John's baptism was not an end in itself, but it prepared the one baptized to look for Jesus Christ to come soon. John's baptism "was the porch that you were to pass through, not the house you were to rest in."[14] Once Christ finished His work to save us and just before He ascended into heaven, He gave the Great Commission, which included the command to baptize in the name of the Father, the Son, and the Holy Ghost (Matthew 28:19-20). This mandate to baptize in the name of our Triune God remains binding until the end of the world. Therefore, once Jesus ascended into heaven and poured out the gift of the Holy Spirit on Pentecost (Acts 2), John's baptism ceased to have any authority. Why? Because it would be senseless to be baptized in order to look for the Messiah to come and die upon the cross and rise again and ascend to heaven when He already had. It appears these disciples in Ephesus were baptized "unto John's baptism" after Christ ascended (probably by Apollos; see Acts 18:24-25), and even after Pentecost; therefore, their baptism carried no biblical validity. They needed to follow the Lord in scriptural baptism that recognized the completed work of the Lord Jesus Christ. This passage shows that one may sincerely submit to baptism, even by immersion, but not be scripturally baptized. Not only must an individual be baptized as a believer by immersion but one must also be baptized by a local church that understands salvation comes by grace through the finished work of Jesus Christ.

Here is what we can do in the city: We can ask people about their salvation, about the work of the Holy Spirit in their lives, and about whether they have been scripturally baptized. Many are sincere but not properly taught. Most people are absolutely confused! We can encourage those with a sincere heart for God, teach them the way of salvation, ask them questions, listen to their questions, and then answer those questions according to Scripture. We can patiently work with them and properly baptize them in the name of the Father, Son, and Holy Spirit and then equip them for ministry. We can work *with* people as the Spirit of God and Word of God work *in* them. We can distribute tracts and find souls hungering for the Word of God. We can proclaim the good news in our neighborhoods and workplaces. We can personally minister to those who come into our church by visiting in their homes. We can personally minister to others by inviting them into our homes. We can personally minister with others by meeting them in a restaurant over good food and listening to their objections and honest questions about God and the Bible.

Ed, an unsaved Jewish man, came to our church with his believing wife. The Lord drew my heart toward Ed. He was going through an extremely difficult time financially when we first met, so he was always happy to meet me for a good hamburger at a diner in the Chelsea area. Being Jewish, he could not understand or believe in the Trinity or the deity of Jesus Christ. I spoke with him, listened to his objections, and answered with the Word of God. Finally, after seven months, Ed trusted in Jesus as His Savior and Lord. This is what God alone can make happen. This is His grace in action.

ORDINARY YOU CAN BOLDLY SPEAK OF GOD'S KINGDOM

Preaching in the shadows of superstition, beside dens of prostitution, Paul was not intimidated by the idolatry and magnificence of the temple of Diana. He "spake boldly for the space of three months, disputing and persuading the things concerning the kingdom of God" (Acts 19:8). Boldness is the confidence and assurance to freely speak. It is forgetting about yourself because you have been with Jesus. Acts 4:13 describes the assurance Peter and John had in their Spirit-filled ministry: "Now when they [the Jewish rulers] saw the boldness of Peter and John, and perceived that they were unlearned and ignorant men, they marvelled; and they took knowledge of them, that they had been with Jesus." The key to boldness is not having a cup of heavily caffeinated coffee, but spending time in the presence of Jesus Christ and asking Him to fill us with His Spirit!

We were having a stewardship banquet at City View Baptist Church, seeking to encourage our people to give toward the purchase of our building. As I walked around the corner of our church to my car, I heard a lady crying for help. I looked up to see a man running toward me on the sidewalk. He was stuffing a pocketbook up his shirt. My detective-like mind went into gear and I quickly recognized that this man was a thief! I thought, "What should I do?" I had only a split second to think. The thing that came to my mind was to stick out my leg and trip him up like they do in the movies. As he was even with me, however, he said, "I have a gun!" For some reason, my leg did not move to trip him! He whizzed past me, and then I looked and saw a man from the neighborhood open his house door to see the commotion. He began to run in my direction toward the thief. "Well, if he will run after this swindler, I will too," I thought. Off I ran, well in front of the other man, right down Flatbush Avenue and past our church, screaming at the top of my lungs, "Stop that thief, stop that thief!" It seemed no one had any desire to stop a thief with a gun. He ran south one block down Flatbush Avenue, turned and ran east one block up Clarendon Road, then turned south down a side street. I continued running after him, shouting all the time, "Stop that thief!" Finally he stopped running, and when he did, so did I! I looked behind me and saw five other men following the thief and me, and they were all on my side. Instinctively, I said, "All right guys, let's get him." I thought I would coordinate the pocketbook recovery effort, although I naturally hesitate getting too close to someone who has a gun. As the thief stopped, he slowly turned around holding the pocketbook in front of him. I carefully approached him; then as we got closer, he dropped the pocketbook at my feet. He ran away. I gathered up the returned goods and triumphantly returned it to the weeping woman back on Vanderveer Place. She expressed her thanks, and others on the block seemed impressed with my efforts. "Good job, Reverend Recker," they said. Two weeks later the lady came by the church and gave us a $50 gift, so I offered my services to her for future emergencies! As I considered my sudden display of boldness while running down Flatbush Avenue shouting at the top of my lungs, "Stop that thief," I was ashamed at my lack of daily boldness concerning the needs of a man's soul. A lady had had her pocketbook stolen with perhaps a few dollars in it, and I was willing to make a fool out of myself. What about the millions of souls in New York City held captive by Satan? Am I willing to be a fool for Christ's sake in order to reach them with the gospel?

Paul displayed daily boldness as he ministered, "disputing and persuading the things concerning the kingdom of God" (Acts 19:8). "Disputing" speaks of discourse with discussion, or of two-way communication.[15] It does not mean Paul argued. "The servant of the Lord must not strive; but be gentle unto all men, apt to teach, patient, in meekness instructing those that oppose themselves" (II Timothy 2:24-25). We must not serve God with a quarrelsome spirit. "Disputing" means there was opportunity for feedback, questions, and answers. This was Paul's method in Thessalonica (Acts 17:2), Athens (Acts 17:17), and Corinth (Acts 18:4). "Persuading" means to bring about a change of mind by the influence of God's Word and God's Spirit in people's lives.[16] These two words tell us of Paul's heart to meet people where they were and persuade them to believe on the Lord Jesus Christ. Jesus Christ is our only hope of a righteous standing before God. We need to love people enough to meet them where they are and then love them too much to let them stay there. This is how God loves you and me. He loved us right where we were, but He loved us too much to let us stay there!

We may not be able to speak *in* the synagogue, but God can work through us to go to the Jewish people with the gospel. We can go into Jewish neighborhoods and boldly speak the things concerning the kingdom of God. Craig Hartman, the founder of a mission board called Shalom Ministries in Brooklyn, New York, is a converted Jewish man with a great desire to reach his people with the gospel. He often shares that in New York City, one out of every seven people we pass on the street is Jewish; more than twice as many Jews live in New York City (1.2 million) than live in Jerusalem (500,000). God can still make witnessing opportunities happen through us. We can witness to those Jewish or Gentile people we meet along the way and reason with them out of the Word of God. We are not responsible for whether they believe, but we are responsible to tell them about our Lord Jesus Christ.

We may never send our sweaty work aprons to others, like Paul did, for healing, but we can rent out schools like he did and use the available means to propagate the Word of God. The price of real estate in Manhattan, or any other large city, is sky-high; we would need at least five million dollars to purchase a suitable building for our church. We can use rented facilities in our large cities at much more reasonable rates to disciple others in the Word of God. I can personally relate to the fact that Paul disputed "daily in the school of one Tyrannus." Our church started in a YMCA on Twenty-third Street. We were forced out of there when they began a construction project, and we moved to a public school (P.S. 33) a few blocks away on Twenty-seventh Street and Ninth Avenue. About a year and a half later, I received a call on a Wednesday afternoon from the head custodian, who told me we could not meet there again. We had to find a new place of worship by that Sunday, plus tell our whole church family. We were kicked out with four days to find a new place of worship! That is not an easy task anywhere, but in Manhattan, it seemed impossible. I went home and claimed Genesis 26:22: "Rehoboth . . . For now the Lord hath made room for us, and we shall be fruitful in the land." I prayed and sent out a number of e-mails requesting prayer for a place where our church could meet. The Lord was more than faithful; by Thursday afternoon (the very next day) we had a better meeting place (it was air-conditioned), with more room, in a private school, for less money. I asked a man in our church who makes signs to make a sign that read "Rehoboth!" for our service that week. This is what God did for us!

ORDINARY YOU CAN MAGNIFY CHRIST'S NAME

"And the name of the Lord Jesus was magnified" as a result of Paul's ministry (Acts 19:17). "Magnify" means to make great. Others realized the greatness of Jesus' character through Paul's ministry. This Scripture demonstrates to us that religion is insufficient to meet the needs of men. If all religions are valid, the last place Paul would have gone was Ephesus. A popular false religion that captivated a city did not frighten Paul from preaching the power of Jesus' righteous life, bloody substitutionary death, and bodily resurrection. Ephesus was the center of a religion that "all Asia and the world" worshiped (v. 27). At the heart of this false religion was Diana. It was this name that was great in the hearts and minds of many in Ephesus. They would later shout, "Great is Diana." Paul's message was "Great is Jesus." Both could not be true.

We see that the greatness of our God is in Him and in who He is and in what He does not in buildings or idols. Jesus can be magnified even when the biggest temple in town is for Diana! Paul did not try to out-build the temple of Diana. Paul did not say, "The temple of Diana is 420 feet long; our church will be 440 feet long! The temple to Diana has 127 columns 60 feet high; we will have 150 columns 70 feet high!" No. Jesus was magnified because God's Word prevailed and conquered the hearts of people in Ephesus.

Because Jesus is not worshiped and magnified, missions exists. Because His name is not glorified, there is a great motive for missions. John Piper in his article "Let the Nations Be Glad" says,

> Missions is not the ultimate goal of the church. Worship is. Missions exists because worship doesn't. Worship is the ultimate, not missions, because God is ultimate, not man. When this age is over, and the countless millions of the redeemed fall on their faces before the throne of God, missions will be no more. It is a temporary necessity. But worship abides for ever.[17]

Missions exists because the name of Jesus Christ is not great in hearts. Missions exists in New York City because people think all kinds of other things are great, rather than Jesus. Missions exists because His praise doesn't sound forth from every tongue.

Paul accomplished more in two years and three months in Ephesus than most men accomplish in a lifetime. I confess that I am personally baffled about how to explain or duplicate it. In two short years all Asia heard about the Lord Jesus Christ. In two short years much people in Asia were persuaded to follow the Lord Jesus Christ. In two short years Paul's ministry threatened the temple and worship of Diana as well as the economic base of that city. I am amazed with this ministry in Ephesus, and I hunger to have even a portion of the blessing in New York City that Paul had in Ephesus. However, I must not think that our church must endanger the economy before I am "successful." This may surprise you, but if our church offerings are high, Wall Street does not quake! I have tracked this carefully and have discovered that if our offerings go up, the Dow Jones Industrial Average does not necessarily go down. I also confess that a part of me would love to stir up such controversy that a riot would result. It would be spiritually exciting, but God has not called us to create controversy but to "earnestly contend *(agonizomai)* for the faith which was once delivered unto the saints" (Jude 3).

Our churches in New York City have been relatively small. We can still have as our goal the glory of God. We can minister so that others will come to know the name of Jesus Christ and glory in Him. We can fulfill the Great Commission by supporting missionaries. We minister realizing that God brings forth the increase. We can continue, tenaciously looking unto Jesus, praying, and seeking our God to do great and mighty things.

On Sundays we have an hour-long live radio ministry that reaches out across northern New Jersey, all of New York City, eastern Long Island, and southern Connecticut. After a thirty-minute message, I take phone calls for about thirty minutes. One night a man called quite angry. He asked me if I believe that one must believe Jesus is God in order to be saved. He then commented that I was creating fear, even in young children. He told me that the gospel of Jesus Christ evokes fear in people and that Jesus did not come to spread fear but love. I then asked him if he believed that Jesus taught the doctrine of eternal damnation.

He skirted my question and then angrily said, "You are going around scaring people. Who are you to be so unloving, because you have no right to do that!"

I said, "Jesus said, 'Fear not them which kill the body, but are not able to kill the soul: but rather fear him which is able to destroy both soul and body in hell'" (Matthew 10:28).

I was able to use that discussion to proclaim that the way to heaven is a strait gate indeed, and it is a loving thing to preach the salvation of grace through Jesus Christ's righteousness alone! Jesus was not spreading fear when He preached that the way to hell is a wide gate through which many go. Jesus spoke the truth in love; so must we.

The week after that phone call, a thirteen-year-old girl called our program and I shared the gospel with her. After the program she professed faith in Jesus over the telephone, and then she said, "My cousin wants to talk with you." After speaking to her, she also professed faith in the Lord Jesus Christ! God alone knows the heart and whether their professions were real, but as we magnify the name of Jesus Christ, the Word of God will grow and prevail. We can see people turn from their sin and destroy their idols, their rock and rap albums, and their wicked videos. We can all magnify Jesus Christ. This is our highest duty and main purpose for living—to glorify and magnify our great God.

We can see people make open, life-changing decisions, sacrificing their idols and wicked deeds to the Lord. These new believers in Acts 19 were so changed that they brought their books and idols, many of them no doubt associated with the temple of Diana, and burned them before all men. The price of those things was fifty thousand pieces of silver. That is fifty thousand days of wages. If you convert this to today's wages in our economy, you will discover that this was well over two million dollars. These books were costly and greatly desired. They were handwritten and rare.

We can see God's Word prevail. We can see homosexuals and lesbians turn from their sinful ways. We can see former adulterers and fornicators come to Christ. We can see atheists believe. We can see thieves born again. We can see these things because God can make them happen. A city church is a "such were" kind of place (I Corinthians 6:11)! Perhaps you are holding on to things that you ought to surrender and burn. You will never be able to magnify Jesus until you first burn your idols. How many of your idols should you give up? Give up all of them. As Hudson Taylor wrote concerning his surrender to God in China, "Let there be no reservation. Give yourself up wholly and fully to Him whose you are and whom you wish to serve in this work, and there can be no disappointment. But once let the question arise, 'Are we called to give up this or that?';

once admit the thought, 'I did not expect such and such inconvenience or privation,' and your service will cease to be that free and happy one which is most conducive to efficiency and success."[18] Only when we surrender all without reservation to our God can we then live without disappointment!

Are you willing to let God work through you and make things happen for His glory? We may not have the wide influence Paul had, but God can use us to magnify the name of the Lord Jesus, boldly speak of God's kingdom, and minister to hungry souls! Our responsibility is to plant and water the seed in great urban areas like Ephesus, and it is God's work to bring forth the increase of the seed. God can use ordinary you in the city!

---

[1]Harvie Conn, "The Kingdom of God and the City of Man," in *Discipling the City,* ed. Roger Greenway (Grand Rapids: Baker Book House, 1992), p. 260.

[2]Roger S. Greenway and Timothy M. Monsma, *Cities: Missions' New Frontier* (Grand Rapids: Baker Book House, 2000), p. 67.

[3]Conn, p. 260.

[4]Conn, p. 261.

[5]Conn, p. 268.

[6]For the phrase "signs and wonders" see also John 4:48; Matthew 12:38; Acts 2:22, 43; Acts 4:30; Acts 5:12. Signs and wonders were done by the Lord Jesus Christ and the apostles, and will be done by the Lord in the heavens and earth at the time of His coming (Acts 2:19; Joel 2:30).

[7]Jim Cymbala, *Fresh Wind, Fresh Fire* (Grand Rapids: Zondervan Publishing House, 1997), p. 138.

[8]Jim Cymbala, *Fresh Power* (Grand Rapids: Zondervan Publishing House, 2001), p. 26.

[9]Cymbala, pp. 58, 59.

[10]Cymbala, p. 59.

[11]Fred Moritz, *Contending for the Faith* (Greenville, S.C.: Bob Jones University Press, 2000), p. 60.

[12]Moritz, pp. 62, 63.

[13]Matthew Henry, *Matthew Henry's Commentary* (McLean, Va.: MacDonald Publishing Company, n.d.), p. 245.

[14]Henry, p. 245.

[15]W. E. Vine, Merrill F. Unger, William White Jr., *Vine's Complete Expository Dictionary of Old and New Testament Words* (Nashville: Thomas Nelson Publishers, 1985), pp. 172, 175.

[16]Vine, p. 469.

[17]John Piper, "Let the Nations Be Glad," in *Perspectives on the World Christian Movement,* ed. by Ralph Winter and Steven Hawthorne (Pasedena, Cal.: William Carey Library, 1999), p. 49.

[18]Howard Taylor and Mrs. Taylor, *J. Hudson Taylor: God's Man in China* (Chicago: Moody Press, 1978), p. 187.

CHAPTER 12

Church Planting in the City

Urban church planting is not hard but it takes hard work. One must be committed in his love and devotion to God. The urban church planter's heart needs to burn with a love for God's righteousness that overflows upon the people to whom he ministers. The urban church planter must pray every step of the way. He must be filled with the Holy Spirit in order to witness to those he contacts. He must study long hours to prepare messages that will feed the flock. He must proceed confidently, knowing that the Word of God has many examples of churches being planted in key population centers that are essentially the same as the modern-day megacity: Rome, Ephesus, Antioch, Corinth, Ephesus, Thessalonica, and Philippi to name a few. Finally, the urban church planter must maintain focus and keep things simple. Following "the list" will help in this area. Keep reading and you will discover what I mean.

PREPARING: BELIEVE GOD PROVIDES

The first stage of church planting is *preparing*. In this period of preparation, you must firmly believe God provides. All you have of a church at this point is the vision in your heart. You have no money. You have no building. You have no people to hear you preach. You have a heavenly dream in your soul that drives you forward to your goal of establishing a church in the midst of souls who desperately need the Lord Jesus Christ.

The first goal during this preparatory stage is raising prayer and financial support to sustain you, the church planter, in your ministry. This time has often been termed "deputation," conveying negative attitudes and injecting many with the fear of "years of travel." Recently the friendly phrase "pre-field ministry" has been used. However you express it, the need for prayer and financial support exists. The church planter requires monthly support for daily needs and also a cash fund for initial expenses.

One of the keys to a pre-field ministry rests in having a strong home church of your own. You must be centered in a good church that sees God's calling upon your life. If those closest to you in your home church do not share your enthusiasm to establish a church in an urban setting, then how can you convince those you do not know of your burden? Work closely with the pastor and members of your home church in all details related to your church-planting desire. How thankful I am for Calvary Baptist Church in Derby, Kansas, and for the faithful pastor, Kent Holcomb. During the summer of 1981 I worked with Pastor Holcomb and did my church internship under his leadership. The Lord cemented a firm friendship between us so that he gladly offered any assistance to help us get to New York City. This church ordained me into the gospel ministry in 1984. Work to build a meaningful relationship with the pastor of your home church. Meet with him to get his counsel and advice. Respect his leadership and build a friendship with him. Share your dream with him. Let him see clearly what God has put in your heart. Have him write a letter of recommendation for you to include in your communications with churches you will contact for meetings.

During this stage, write "the list" of things you will need in establishing a new church. Write a tentative budget for your family in the city of your ministry. If possible, find out what it costs to live, eat, drive in the city you will enter. Call some pastors or people you know in that city. How much is rent? How much is car insurance? How high are the utility bills? Next, enumerate on another list the various things you will purchase to establish a church. Make these your prayer requests. After I left the church we started in Brooklyn, I made a list of things we needed for the next church we planned to begin. This list included the rental of a church building and home, a church sign, church brochures, hymnals, chairs, a pulpit, visitor cards, decision cards, offering envelopes, bulletins, choir music, and a sound system. Whenever anyone asked me if I needed anything, I showed my list. One church donated money for our church sign. Another church gave us hymnals. Along the way, I bought some of the small yet essential items like visitor cards and offering envelopes. I remember buying visitor cards one day well before the start of our services, and it gave me joy thinking that a visitor to our church would one day write his name on that card. My vision was enlarged on account of that small purchase.

The second matter of consideration during the period of preparation is to obtain meetings in churches. Contact churches in writing six months in advance of when you want to present your work. Include a resume and a letter of recommendation from your pastor. Also, share your purpose, goals, and strategy for the church you will establish. Be brief or no one will read your material. Within two weeks of your letter, call the church by phone and seek to arrange a meeting. Be confident and assured without being pushy. When we began our deputation, I did not know many churches. I obtained lists of churches from Pastor Holcomb, and our mission board supplied us with lists of churches in various areas. My home church was in Kansas, so that is where we began our deputation. I contacted churches that Pastor Holcomb knew and obtained several meetings through his recommendation. I served at Grace Baptist Church in Landrum, S.C., as a youth director during my graduate studies at Bob Jones University. The pastor assisted me in obtaining some meetings with churches he knew. Some of these churches still support us in New York City. I once wrote about thirty-five churches in the Michigan area. I did not personally know any of those pastors or churches. I prayed over those letters and sent them off. A week later I began calling the various pastors. I quickly discovered the difficulty of reaching a pastor in his office! Of those thirty-five letters, I obtained two meetings. At times the process discouraged me, but I did not quit. I sought to be aggressive without being pushy.

We developed a puppet ministry that could be used in junior church. Our "New York City Puppet Gang" opened doors for us to get into churches that otherwise would not have had us come. Most pastors do not want to surrender their pulpit on Sunday morning, so we always volunteered to serve in junior church with our New York City puppets. Debbie made the puppets out of felt and socks. We called them Vinny, Jermaine, and Louie the Rat. She also taught others how to make puppets because people young and old love them. Years later people would ask us about our puppets. Sadly, I had to tell them they met up with a New York City fate: they were stolen out of our car in Brooklyn one evening while we were on visitation!

During my last semester at Bob Jones University, as I worked on my master's degree, I spent spare minutes between classes and time during work breaks calling churches around the country. My goal was to hit the road raising up prayer and financial support immediately upon graduation in May. I set up an itinerary from June through December.

I remember calling the church near Clemson University where I was saved as a freshman college student. The Welcome Baptist Church was small, and Pastor Earnest Childs did not know me, for he had not been ministering at that church when the Lord saved me. I called him while on break at a lumber supply store where I worked. He said that they could not have me present our work. Their small church already supported a significant number of missionaries. The conversation ended, and I went back to work. About fifteen minutes later, he called me back with a change of heart and told me, "If you cannot get a meeting in the church where you were saved, you cannot get a meeting anywhere!" My heart sang with joy. Debbie and I went to Welcome Baptist to present our church-planting desire for our first-ever deputation meeting while I was still in graduate school. I stood in the church where my spiritual life began to begin a new life as a church planter. We had a wonderful day. After the Sunday evening service, I asked the pastor if he had any suggestions. Did he ever! He said, "You need to put your slide presentation on tape." I had narrated it verbally. "Next," he said, "you need to make a sturdy display that will withstand the punishment of constant travel." I had a flimsy, cardboard display. "Last, you need to get about three good messages that will present your burden for the city." Needless to say, I felt like a failure after this first meeting, but I attempted to do what he had advised. I recorded our slide presentation in a studio, and I made a sturdy wood display. I am still working on three good messages! After this meeting, Pastor Childs wrote a letter I still treasure. He said, "It was a real joy to have you with us for your first deputation meeting. Many of our folks expressed their appreciation for your messages and your anticipated ministry in New York City. You are embarking upon the most difficult aspect of missionary service—deputation—but don't let it scare you and don't become discouraged. The Devil will cast his fiery darts of fear, unbelief, bitterness and self-pity, so keep the shield of faith in place and encourage yourself in the Lord." These timeless words still challenge me to go forward and attempt to accomplish the dreams God has put in my heart.

As you travel to raise prayer and financial support, befriend the pastor of the church you are visiting. The pastors I have met during our travels continue to be my best friends in the ministry. Also, do whatever they ask of you. In one New England church, the pastor asked me to show my slides and give a ten-minute testimony. My heart burned to preach, but he did not ask me to preach. I did not complain about it, either. I gladly accepted his offer, and he told me the next morning they would support us $100 per month. He also confided that the last missionary they had had complained about giving only a ten minute testimony.

FINDING: BELIEVE GOD DIRECTS

The second aspect in church planting is the *finding* stage. You must trust God for direction. At this point, you have your support and you sit in your car in the middle of the city you seek to reach. Where will you live? Where will your church be? You must find a place to live and minister.

I recommend you prayerfully call the pastors in the area. In each of the three churches we established, I did not discover where we would minister on my own solely through prayer! I spoke to respected men of God. They understood things I did not about their communities. Before we started our first church in Flatbush, Brooklyn, Pastor Jerry Walker, a good friend to all of the Independent Baptist pastors in the city, drove me around the very area where our church would later begin.

I remember wondering where to go after leaving our Brooklyn church. I had prayed for God's leading; then I called Pastor Paul McCardel from Queens. I asked him, "Where does a great need for a church exist in Queens?" He told me about the Jamaica area. By divine providence, I knew someone in that area who had been a member of our Brooklyn church, and I knew she wanted a church closer to her home. That phone call directed me like an arrow to the southeast part of Queens, where Parkway Baptist Church eventually was established.

When we were leaving Parkway, I went to a pastors' luncheon at a diner. A young man I had never seen before or since sat across from me at the table. I mentioned casually my desire to start a church in Manhattan. This young man said, "You should start a church in the Chelsea area." I wrote down the location of Chelsea, and when I started surveying communities in Manhattan, my heart leaped with excitement as I walked through Chelsea. Our church now meets in the Chelsea-Greenwich Village area of Manhattan. I cannot say it strongly enough: get counsel and advice from other pastors.

Another step in finding where God would have you begin a ministry is to survey the various areas you have in mind. Get to know the city. Drive around. Walk up and down the streets. Pray as you go. Buy a map and a notebook. Write down observations. Obtain census or population figures from the chamber of commerce. Search out your city on the World Wide Web. In a way similar to Nehemiah scouting out the city of Jerusalem without telling anyone what was in his heart, assess and examine the area. Here are some questions to consider and answer in seeking the direction of God to a particular area.

1. What is the culture of the people in the targeted community?
2. What languages are spoken?
3. Has there been a recent shift in culture?
4. What are the conditions of the families in the area?
5. Are there private homes or apartment buildings?
6. What are the social issues that influence and affect the area?
7. What kinds of churches already exist in the area, and where are they?

Once you determine the general area where you will begin the church, find a place to live. Settle your wife and children into an apartment or house. Do not feel guilty about taking the necessary time to fix up your living place. We have sometimes had to do extensive cleaning, painting, and repairing before we could move into a rented apartment or house. In a large city, a wife needs her husband to help her adjust to the new culture. Go to the grocery store together. Walk around the neighborhood together. Pray together and allow a sense of excitement for the potential church to grip your wife and children for the potential church. This enthusiasm will not happen if they are not happy with their home.

In 1993, God allowed us to purchase a wood-frame house in Rosedale, Queens. Debbie found the house through a realtor. We bought the house when interest rates were rock bottom; God has blessed us with a beautiful home. Actually, it was not beautiful when we bought it, but we have gutted and renovated the bathroom, sanded the wood floors, Sheetrocked, installed a new kitchen counter and sink, insulated and refurbished the attic into a bedroom, waterproofed the basement, and installed new windows, vinyl siding, and a new roof. I did most of the work. Now we have a beautiful house! All the nations of the world live in our neighborhood, with the majority of people being West Indian or Hispanic. Older white people live here too, but as they die, first generation immigrants from Saint Lucia, Guyana, Puerto Rico, the Dominican Republic, or Jamaica take their place. Our block actually is very quiet and peaceful most of the time. It is not what you picture New York City to be in your mind. One of the nicest things about our home is the big brick house across the street. That home elevates our whole block and makes the five simple wood-frame homes on the other side of the street, of which ours is one, look much nicer.

Next, the church planter must locate a facility where the new church can assemble. You can share a building by using a Seventh-day Adventist church, the banquet room of a restaurant, a day-care center, a public school, a Veterans of Foreign Wars building, or some other kind of building. Our Manhattan church, Heritage Baptist Church, began in a YMCA on Twenty-third Street and Eighth Avenue in the Chelsea area of Manhattan. We rented two rooms: one for our adult meetings, and the other for our Sunday school and junior church. I know one church planter who started a church in a Brooklyn barbershop.

When I started our Brooklyn church, City View Baptist, I actually tried to locate a day-care center in which to start. I requested to use a day-care center on the corner of Flatbush Avenue and Vanderveer Place in the heart of Flatbush, Brooklyn. As I stood at the door of this day-care center, a pleasant Jamaican woman told me she would have to speak to her husband and that he would get back to me. This was my first glimmer of hope. The next day I received a call from her husband. Not only did he own the day-care center but also the adjacent storefront building. The Seventh-day Adventists rented the downstairs, but they were also using the upstairs rent-free. He proposed to me that I could rent the upstairs from Sunday through Friday evening. He told me that the Adventist group used the upstairs for their "Sabbath school." I countered, "If the Adventists use what we are renting on Saturday, we should be able to use what *they* are renting on *Sunday*!" This sounded logical to him. He then made an offer of rent for $350 per month. I did not know this was a tremendous price, so I haggled with him and brought him down to $325. He agreed, and I wrote him a check for $650. This included one month's rent as security and one month's rent. It was also evident that he and the Seventh-day Adventist pastor did not like one another. Although he was an Adventist himself, he did not attend this church. He felt he had done them a great favor in renting them his building for almost nothing, and they showed little appreciation in return. He and I became friends right away. He spoke to the Adventist group and told them that if they wanted to continue using the upstairs for their educational ministry, they must allow us to use their church auditorium. What a miracle! I had wondered, "Where am I going to get a piano, a pulpit, chairs, and everything else one needs to begin church services?" Here I was coming to one of the highest-priced cities in the world to start a church, and I had very little money. God provided and led the way. After one year that Adventist congregation moved, so we rented the entire building and eventually bought that building.

You can also pray and seek to rent your own building. If financially possible, this arrangement carries more advantages. It provides instant identity in the community. You can put up a sign that advertises your church twenty-four hours a day. It gives the church flexibility; you can have midweek services when you want. You can have vacation Bible schools in the summer and evangelistic meetings, mission conferences, and other special meetings more easily. Starting with your own facility also allows for uniformity; all your services occur in the same place. As I write this, our Manhattan church meets for Sunday morning services in a private school, but our Wednesday night prayer fellowships and Heritage Discipleship Institute meet in a YMCA. Having a variety of meeting places adds confusion to a church calendar. When we planted Parkway Baptist Church in Jamaica, Queens, we began in a rented storefront. This gave us immediate identity in the neighborhood and allowed our church to grow to two morning services by our second year. In each of the three churches that I have started, I paid the first month's rent, but the church through the regular offerings was able to bear its own expense once we started our regular worship services.

SEEKING: BELIEVE GOD OPENS HEARTS

The third part of starting a church can be called *seeking for souls*. In this stage, be confident that God will open hearts. Just as God opened Lydia's heart in Philippi and led Paul to the jailer, so God prepares hearts and leads us to those who need to hear the gospel.

I remember the words that rang in my ears as I sat in our second floor apartment in Windsor Terrace, Brooklyn, in September of 1984. "What do I do now?" Those words bombarded my spirit. I had traveled for over a year telling every church in which I preached that I would be a church planter in New York City. I would go into a needy area in New York City, establish a church, then move on to another needy area and begin again. Was I crazy for telling them that? While I was considering what to do, I discovered "the list." I wandered over to my file cabinet and picked out my notes that said "Church Planting." I thought, "Maybe this will give me some practical advice on what I am supposed to do." I skimmed through the notes to find out what steps I was to take in starting a church in this concrete jungle known as New York City! I came to a part that stated, "Pre-planning prior to services." That sounded good. The first point said, "Be certain of God's will." I was sure that I was in the place God wanted. Next it said, "Train for church planting." I had done that, or so I thought. The third point said, "Select an area or city." I had done that, too. I went to the next item, for I was already in the city! "Draw up a constitution and decide on a style of church brochure" were the next two points. These had also been done. As I read these things, I became thankful for my education at Bob Jones University and for Dr. Otis Holmes, who had taught my church planting class. I felt God had called me and trained me, and I had written a church constitution and church brochure in my church planting class. I went to the next main section, still looking for practical help on what to do in order to start a church. I found the part that said what to do on your first week on the field. "Rent a home or apartment" was on the top of the list. We had done that. God had clearly directed us to our Brooklyn apartment. The apartment had been vacant for some time and needed basic cosmetic work. Debbie and I prayed concerning God's will for us, and we felt a strong peace that we should live there. We moved into it in June of 1984 and continued our deputation while we adjusted to city life. Our neighborhood was safe and friendly, howbeit segregated. New York City is not always the melting pot it is made out to be. Sometimes it is more like a "marble pot." My neighbor Bernie spoke to me one day and said, "We are all Archie Bunkers around here. This neighborhood is 'lily white,' and we are going to keep it that way!" Those certainly were not my sentiments, but there was no use arguing with him. He resembled the television character Archie Bunker in more ways than one.

I would drive around Brooklyn and wonder, "How can we crack this city? How do I begin?" It was huge. There were multitudes of people. Everyone looked so busy. Churches large and small seemed to sit on every corner. Roman Catholic churches owned blocks of city real estate. A seemingly infinite number of smaller churches met in storefronts. I was intimidated, but I kept my focus and returned to the list. It said, "Open bank accounts." Here was something that I had not done, and it was not hard, so I strolled up to Ninth Avenue and opened our first account in New York City while other customers seemed to blow cigarette smoke at me from every direction. I walked out of the bank smelling like a Marlboro and went back to my list. "Investigate area seriously for possible meeting places." The list was becoming more difficult, but I set out to find a place. I bought a map of New York City and began to drive up and down the streets. I stopped at VFW buildings, day-care centers, and even a building where people practiced yoga. After a week or so of searching, I found the storefront building on Flatbush Avenue. I did not know much about the neighborhood. I did not know that two blocks from the building was an area called "crack heaven." I did not know the neighborhood was 90 percent black, mostly Caribbean. We secured the building for a great price, and I went back to my list. In retrospect I confess great naiveté but in my heart there was tremendous satisfaction as I sensed the leading of God.

The list said to get our church brochures printed. It was early October, so I set November 18 for our first service. My father was a printer, so I sent him the format of our brochure, and within a week I had five thousand brochures. I stamped on every brochure "Our first service is November 18." I went back to the list and the next point was, "Pass them out, stupid!"

With brochures in hand, I hit the streets to distribute them. This season of time spent in seeking after souls is an exciting few months. You feel like you are going out on a limb and you must trust God to keep you from falling as you seek for fruit that will remain. There is a growing anticipation as to what God will do on that first Sunday. I began going door to door, and street corner to street corner. The first day out, I came to the corner of Bedford Avenue and Avenue D and the Lord led me to speak to Carter. I continued visiting and distributing our church brochure. One day I rang a bell and waited and waited. I thought no one was home. Just as I was going to leave, an elderly man came very slowly to the door. I introduced myself to him. His name was Mr. Crandon. The conversation was brief. I walked away thinking, "A nice man, but how would he make it to church? He could hardly make it to the front door!" Little did I know that behind Mr. Crandon was his college-age granddaughter, Pamela. I did not see her, but she listened to our conversation. She initially thought I was a Jehovah's Witness, but she looked over the church brochure and she came to our first service along with her high-school age sister, Kim, and their mother, Yvonne. All three of these ladies believed on the Lord Jesus Christ in our first service at City View Baptist Church! They have continued serving the Lord, and today Pam and Kim's nieces are also baptized members of the church.

As our first service approached, the excitement in my heart grew. In the Flatbush area there are many four- to six-floor apartment buildings. I would take the elevator to the top floor and work my way down distributing our brochure. Graffiti often covered the walls of the elevators and hallways. The stench of urine filled the air in the stairwells. When I knocked, people would not even open their doors. They looked through peepholes and answered "Who?" Looking at their enlarged eye and smiling, I would respond, "My name is Matthew Recker from City View Baptist Church." They would often say, "What?" If dogs lived in other apartments on that floor, they would bark and make all kinds of noise. I learned to laugh to keep from going crazy. I soon discovered the best way to reach those in the apartment buildings was simply to slip the brochure under the doors. Those interested could call or visit the church.

On Halloween I received a call from an angry woman. "How did you get my name?" was the first thing she said to me as I picked up the phone. "What do you mean?" I said. "You put something under my door and it had my name on it." I tried to keep the conversation going in a more friendly direction. She was upset! Seeking to calm her down, I responded, "Miss, I did put something under your door, but it did not have your name on it." She was persistent. "I am holding it right here in my hand, and it has my name on it!" I said, "Please look again to make sure." She opened up the brochure and then with shock said, "Oh, it doesn't have my name on it." Where I stamped the brochure with the day of our first service, she thought I had put her name on it. She calmed down instantly, and the Lord opened up a door of conversation. Her name was Laura. She lived in an apartment building with her twelve-year-old daughter, Johanny, and four-year-old daughter, Demaris. Her husband had run off from her. She had tried religion with the Unification Church but had left that false movement. She had contemplated suicide. She had thought her name appeared on the brochure because her friend from the Unification church had told her to visit a Baptist church because Baptists preach the Bible. That night I spoke to Laura and told her of the love and righteousness of Jesus Christ, and she believed on the Lord right over the phone! The next day, Debbie and I went to visit her, encouraged her, and began to disciple her in her new faith. She grew and she also came to our first service.

The day of our first service arrived. I woke up at 5:00 A.M. and went to the church to clean, set up our sound system, and put out our hymnbooks. Dr. Marvin Lewis, the director of our mission board, along with his wife, drove up from Greenville to be in our first service. We had over fifty people attend. Laura was there, along with Yvonne, Pam, and Kim. Our landlady, Ginny, came with her sister, Frances, and her son, Andrew. A drunkard I met named Gene attended. A lady deeply involved in crack also visited. The following week twenty-four people attended, and from there we grew. God began to lead us to people who needed the Lord and others who were saved but needed a good Bible-believing church to attend. We started weekly Bible clubs with the many children from the community. God blessed and the church grew gradually and consistently.

After the Adventist church moved out and we began renting the whole building, we began living in the upstairs apartment. I would tell people we had a parking meter in our front yard. This was my first experience of many in building and Sheetrocking a wall, as we sectioned off the upstairs to make a bedroom for our children. In March 1987, the owner of the building said to me, "I am moving to Florida and must sell this building. Would you like to buy it?" He told me the price: $200,000. I agreed. He said, "Can you get the down payment of $50,000 by next month?" I was shocked, but I remained composed. Our church had only about $4,000 in savings. With a confidence that was not from me, I said, "We can have the money by January 1, 1988." That began a time in which we saw God provide miraculously. Just after that, a dear lady from Arkansas sent our church $250 and said it was her earnings from a garage sale she had had. From that point on, I just knew God could provide the funds, and He did. Our church bought the building, and that was a great step toward our planting an indigenous church.

As time passes, pray for your church to grow. Work to get people to visit the church by continuing to evangelize, distributing attractive church brochures, and encouraging those who visit the church to bring their friends. Encourage people who visit to return. Call them on the phone, write letters, meet them for meals, invite them into your home, and visit the homes of those who attend. Get involved with people! Preach messages that feed the people. Discover their spiritual condition and help them grow. Lead the lost to salvation, teach those not baptized to follow in obedience, and disciple those in the church through personal Bible studies. As visitors become regular attenders, pastor them to become members of the church. Delegate responsibility to faithful believers, and plan for times of church fellowship so that meaningful relationships can be established. Give members a sense of ownership of the church. As people develop relationships and get involved in ministry, they will stay. As people develop a sense that the church is their church, they will remain whether the church planter does or not.

In establishing a church in the city, you must pray all the way while walking in the Spirit. Believe that God provides, God directs, and God opens hearts! As you take the steps to start a church, have "the list" to help you prepare yourself, find the place, and seek for souls.

As you behold the city, I pray that God will give you a burden for the great urban areas of the world. Behold the city in the Scripture. As you read God's Word, allow passages related to cities in the Bible to burn in your heart. Meditate upon and memorize those Bible verses. Study what the Bible says about the city by using commentaries and Bible dictionaries. Remember that the city has not changed. Behold the city by praying for modern urban areas. Find missionaries or churches that need prayer, in cities from Boston to Bombay. Write them, e-mail them, and look up their web-site to find out more about their ministries. Behold the city with a personal visit. See a city first-hand by making your next vacation a trip to the city. Contact a good church beforehand and come to the city with a servant's heart. Be willing to be a voice for the Lord in the city by distributing tracts, setting up a prayer station, singing a special song, or teaching a class in an urban church. God's people may even consider moving to the city to serve the Lord in varied capacities. The opportunities for ministry in the local church are endless. God's presence and power can sustain you in the city so that you can conquer fear. Behold the city, and God can use ordinary you to win the lost, disciple individuals, encourage believers, or establish a church in a metropolitan area of our world for His glory.

Christ for the Crisis

For further information
see
www.christforthecrisis.com